Supporting Educational Transitions for Ages 3–19

Also Available from Bloomsbury

Pedagogy, Politics and Philosophy of Peace, edited by
Carmel Borg and Michael Grech
Pedagogies of Taking Care, Dennis Atkinson
Wonder and Education, Anders Schinkel
Raymond Williams and Education, Ian Menter
Critical Pedagogy for Healing, edited by Tricia M. Kress,
Christopher Emdin and Robert Lake
Hopeful Pedagogies in Higher Education, edited by Mike Seal
Children, Religion and the Ethics of Influence, John Tillson
Socially Just Pedagogies, edited by Vivienne Bozalek, Rosi Braidotti, Tamara
Shefer and Michalinos Zembylas
Critical Human Rights, Citizenship, and Democracy Education,
edited by Michalinos Zembylas and André Keet

Supporting Educational Transitions for Ages 3–19

Edited by Elizabeth Gregory and
Liz Stevenson

BLOOMSBURY ACADEMIC
LONDON • NEW YORK • OXFORD • NEW DELHI • SYDNEY

BLOOMSBURY ACADEMIC
Bloomsbury Publishing Plc, 50 Bedford Square, London, WC1B 3DP, UK
Bloomsbury Publishing Inc, 1359 Broadway, New York, NY 10018, USA
Bloomsbury Publishing Ireland, 29 Earlsfort Terrace, Dublin 2, D02 AY28, Ireland

BLOOMSBURY, BLOOMSBURY ACADEMIC and the Diana logo are
trademarks of Bloomsbury Publishing Plc

First published in Great Britain 2026

Copyright © Elizabeth Gregory, Liz Stevenson, and Contributors 2026

Elizabeth Gregory and Liz Stevenson have asserted their right under the Copyright,
Designs and Patents Act, 1988, to be identified as Editors of this work.

Cover Design by Megan Wilson
Cover images © Lily and Icons-Studio via Adobe Stoc

All rights reserved. No part of this publication may be: i) reproduced or transmitted in
any form, electronic or mechanical, including photocopying, recording or by means of
any information storage or retrieval system without prior permission in writing from
the publishers; or ii) used or reproduced in any way for the training, development or
operation of artificial intelligence (AI) technologies, including generative AI technologies.
The rights holders expressly reserve this publication from the text and data mining
exception as per Article 4(3) of the Digital Single Market Directive (EU) 2019/790.

Bloomsbury Publishing Plc does not have any control over, or responsibility for, any
third-party websites referred to or in this book. All internet addresses given in this
book were correct at the time of going to press. The author and publisher regret
any inconvenience caused if addresses have changed or sites have ceased
to exist, but can accept no responsibility for any such changes.

A catalogue record for this book is available from the British Library.

A catalog record for this book is available from the Library of Congress.

ISBN: HB: 978-1-3504-7169-6
       PB: 978-1-3504-7168-9
     ePDF: 978-1-3504-7171-9
    eBook: 978-1-3504-7170-2

Typeset by Integra Software Services Pvt. Ltd.
Printed and bound in Great Britain

For product safety related questions contact productsafety@bloomsbury.com.

To find out more about our authors and books visit www.bloomsbury.com
and sign up for our newsletters.

Contents

List of Figures	vi
List of Tables	vii
List of Contributors	viii
Foreword *Emma Turner*	xi
Preface *Elizabeth Gregory and Liz Stevenson*	xiii

Part 1 Academic Curriculum

1	Transition into Early Years *Mandy Pierlejewski and Jennifer Holly*	3
2	Transitions to Primary *Liz Stevenson*	21
3	Transitions to Secondary *Liz Stevenson*	41
4	Transitions to Tertiary: Post-16 Education *Elizabeth Gregory*	57
5	International Perspectives *Divya Jindal-Snape*	75

Part 2 Holistic Approaches

6	SEND and the Role of SENCOs *Lorraine Petersen*	93
7	Engaging Families and Communities in the Transition Process *Claire Wilkinson*	111
8	Behaviour and Integration into School Culture *Karl Rogerson*	127
9	Pastoral Matters and Emotional Wellbeing *Charlotte Bagnall*	147
10	The Impact of Disadvantage on Educational Transitions *Elizabeth Gregory*	165

Index	181

Figures

5.1	Examples of Additional Support Needs (The Education [Additional Support for Learning] [Scotland] Act [2004] [amended 2009])	77
5.2	Impact of key factors on YP's transitions experiences	85
9.1	The design of Talking about School Transitions 5–7 (TaST 5–7)	153

Tables

2.1	Differences between GLD assessments in EYFS and phonics/end of key stage tests	28
2.2	Suggested areas in a classroom	32
3.1	Curriculum links in geography	44
3.2	Differences between primary and secondary school experiences	51
3.3	Considerations for schools' preparation	52

Contributors

Charlotte Bagnall, Dr, is Lecturer at the University of Manchester. Charlotte is an applied social psychologist, with a particular interest in intervention science and co-creation within education, and is a leading expert in school transitions research. Nationally she has been invited as an advisor in the design and evaluation of school transition provision within several Local Education Authorities. Her research has also been referenced in policy guidelines for NICE (07/22) and Health Scotland (01/20). Charlotte is Principal Investigator of the *P-S WELLS* research project and *TaST 5-6* intervention evaluation research project, which she discusses in her chapter.

Elizabeth Gregory, Dr, is Lecturer in Education at the University of Manchester. She has taught in both the FE and the HE sectors and is particularly interested in the impact that academic transition has on learner identity, and in the different perceptions and values attached to different forms of academic accreditation. She has published and spoken widely on the topics of post-16 transitions and qualifications, the impact of disadvantage in educational settings, and the impact of government policy on Teacher Training and on teacher recruitment and retention.

Emma Turner is a school improvement advisor based in the East Midlands. She has served in primary for over 28 years in teaching, leadership, headship, MAT and LA leadership roles and as a specialist consultant in curriculum, research informed practice, and flexible working. She has worked on regional transition projects and regularly works with large stakeholder groups on effective transition. Emma is also a published author of 6 education books, co-host of the Mind the Gap education podcast, primary school chair of governors, keynote speaker, Fellow of the Chartered College of Teaching, and mum of three.

Jennifer Holly is Senior Lecturer in Early Childhood Education at Leeds Beckett University. She has been involved in initial teacher education and education studies in HE for fifteen years, focusing mainly on the three to seven age range. Her recent roles have focused on supporting student transition to higher education alongside teaching pedagogically focused content on an initial teacher education course.

Divya Jindal-Snape is Professor of Education, Inclusion and Life Transitions at the University of Dundee, Scotland. She is Director of the Transformative Change: Educational and Life Transitions (TCELT) Research Centre and leads on the International Network of Transitions Researchers. Her research expertise is in the field of educational and life transitions, inclusion, creativity, health education, voice and comics. Her book most relevant to the current book is *A–Z of Transitions* (2016) which is a reference book providing information about different types of transitions and strategies to facilitate them.

Lorraine Petersen OBE is an independent educational consultant specializing in SEND and Mental Health. Lorraine spent the first twenty-five years of her career as a teacher and headteacher in primary schools within the West Midlands. In 2004 Lorraine was appointed as the CEO of nasen (The National Association for Special Educational Needs) where she worked for nine years. At the end of 2013 Lorraine established her own consultancy business and has been delivering training, advice and support to schools and local authorities. In 2009 Lorraine was awarded an OBE for her services to special education.

Mandy Pierlejewski, Dr, is Senior Lecturer in Early Childhood Education at Leeds Beckett University. She has been involved in initial teacher education for the past ten years, focusing mainly on the three to seven age range. Her main research interest is datafication, where she has focused on the use of the doppelganger as a methodological tool to understand the impact of datafication on subjectivity and pedagogy. She has also published papers focusing on recent changes to initial teacher education in England.

Karl Rogerson is Principal of Billesley Primary School and Director of the Billesley Research School. He has led the school since 2016, guiding it to become an EEF Research School in 2019, where he focuses on evidence-based practices to drive school improvement. Passionate about professional development and developing people, Karl is dedicated to fostering leadership and continuous growth among staff. He is committed to high standards in teaching and learning, especially for disadvantaged pupils. Prior to his current roles, he worked as a curriculum consultant for Birmingham Local Authority, supporting schools in developing effective teaching and learning strategies across the city.

Liz Stevenson is Headteacher at a Special School in Birmingham as well as a consultant in School Improvement with a focus on transition between Key Stages 2 and 3. She is Co-founder of TransitionEd and has had the sole responsibility of the annual conferences since 2023. Her M.Ed. in Educational Leadership focused on transition as well as disadvantaged and parental engagement. You can find more of Liz's work at http://transitionmatters.coach/ [transitionmatters.coach].

Claire Wilkinson is a PhD student with the University of Lincoln and an Assistant Head of Faculty for Religion, Philosophy and Ethics at Aston Academy, UK. Her research interests focus on parental engagement, addressing disadvantage in secondary education and the changing face of inclusion in mainstream secondary education.

Foreword
Emma Turner

When we think about transition it can imply change, new beginnings or even a seismic shift, but what this book is really about is continuity rather than change.

In any journey there are constants, and in any journey through education, the only constant is the child. The curriculum, the location, the pedagogy and the uniform may all be different, but the children we support are the ones who experience all the facets and enactments of our complete educational offer.

Recognizing the need for continuity through change is at the heart of transition, and this book – through its research, diverse and experienced voices, and carefully curated case studies – provides a rich and supportive walk through how to make multiple changes feel seamless and supportive whilst being effective and impactful.

Whether managing a very first move from preschool into formal education, or tackling transition for specific groups, ages and communities, this book is an indispensable guide to the what, the why and the how of transition. Every move a child makes is unique, and what works for one phase or setting is not necessarily transferable to a different context. What this book does beautifully is to acknowledge that throughout a child's development, change management requires a nuanced and specific approach. Through its use of experts in each field and a recognition of each change's unique challenges and circumstances, the approach and focus on transition is turned from the transactional to the transformative.

Getting change right for the children is even more important when set against the backdrop of the multiple changes and hitherto unseen situations in education that have faced pupils and educators since the lockdowns of 2020. The current cohorts of children have already managed more change in their short lives than the sector has seen for decades. Ensuring continuity against a backdrop of multiple changes is even more reason to focus with precision on getting transition right.

Transition is an opportunity to spark excitement about new opportunities, to build on previous learning and successes, a chance to welcome pupils, families and communities into our organizations, and it is also always a moment of hope and possibility. Any transition can be handled positively and successfully; this book provides a detailed overview of how transition can be managed in such a way at each juncture and change so that our children are excited and empowered to take their next steps whatever their previous experience.

Successful transition is also predicated on successful communication. Communication between schools, settings, families, specialist staff, pupils and teachers is woven throughout each chapter as it is only through forming a secure connection between all those who influence the success and wellbeing of a child that we get transition right. I would therefore urge any reader of this book to do so in its entirety, to notice and appreciate the multiple changes and points of transition our pupils go through during their time in education, and how the experiences of one phase influence transition into another. Seeing only our own leg of a journey does not give us a fully rounded picture of our contribution to the educational landscape and so exploring this book in all its fullness is a rare opportunity to glimpse behind the curtain of our children's next or previous act.

As educators we are all one chapter in the children's educational stories, and it is of the utmost importance that we appreciate the narrative in its entirety and ensure that the links between each chapter are coherent, enticing and congruous.

Understanding transition is therefore more than just uniforms and pedagogy, timetables and teachers, or curriculum and kit; it is about understanding the delicate management of change and continuity and remembering that behind the data transfer is a young person about to embark upon a new adventure with us.

Let's get it right, for everyone.

Preface
Elizabeth Gregory and Liz Stevenson

The idea for this book came about in 2022, when Elizabeth attended the annual TransitionEd Conference of which Liz is one of the organizers. The popularity of these conferences and the wide range of speakers and topics involved every year convinced us that there is a market for an accompanying book. One of the conference's unique selling points is its recognition that educators are interested in a wide range of transition issues beyond those specifically affecting their own area of practice, but may not always have the time to seek out and read individual texts to further their knowledge and understanding. In the same way that the conference has presented a range of information in an accessible format from a wide range of contributors over the years, this book aims to offer key points and advice in an easy-to-use format via a series of short, evidence-informed chapters on different stages and aspects of transition.

Supporting Educational Transitions from 3–19 provides a unique perspective on the process of transition to and within a range of educational contexts. The book is aimed at educators, school leaders and education students, and provides research-based evidence on the opportunities and challenges brought by transitions across the educational life course. As educators ourselves with a keen interest in all aspects of transition, we have found a dearth of books that offer a joined-up approach to the transition process. Instead, existing volumes often focus on one particular stage of education (such as Key Stage 2 to Key Stage 3) or one specific aspect of the transition process (such as the challenges faced by international students). We believe that this can lead to a blinkered approach to understanding and supporting transitions that we aim to address by giving an overview of transitions throughout an individual's academic career. We believe this is vital if educators are to understand the whole journey a learner undertakes, rather than just their own particular stop along the way.

The book is divided into two parts. Part One offers a focus on the curriculum as a means of exploring academic aspects of transition from Early Years right up to post-compulsory education. Part Two takes a more holistic approach by considering the social and pastoral elements of transition, including external factors such as disadvantage and parental support. Each chapter presents evidence-based research along with case studies and practical tips and advice that educators can implement in their own practice, as well as suggestions for further reading that will allow readers to follow up on any areas of interest. The book is predominantly focused on the education system in England, although parallels are drawn with other countries throughout and there will be much of relevance here to international readers.

Part One begins with an illuminating discussion of transitions into the Early Years from Mandy Pierlejewski and Jennifer Holly, two former Early Years teachers who are now teacher educators. They outline the broad scope of Early Years Foundation Stage (EYFS) provision in England along with the statutory guidance which governs this provision, and highlight the roles played by communities, teachers and school leaders in supporting the transitions of our youngest learners. Liz Stevenson then contributes two chapters on transitions later in the school journey, examining the moves to primary and to secondary. She explores the array of differences that children and young people experience in the move from EYFS through to KS3 across the two chapters, considering how children may feel during these transitions and how schools can best support them through this process.

Transitions to Post-16 education are explored by Elizabeth Gregory in Chapter 4, which examines both 16–19 education and transitions to university. These very different sectors nevertheless offer similar challenges and opportunities by requiring learners to develop increasing independence in both their studies and lives outside of education. Part One closes with a fascinating overview of International Perspectives on Primary to Secondary transitions from Divya Jindal-Snape, in which she highlights commonalities and differences across a number of education systems, and shares some of her world-leading research as well as drawing upon a range of other findings from across the globe.

Part Two examines a range of more holistic challenges and approaches, beginning with the crucial topic of supporting learners with Special Education Needs and Disabilities (SEND) and the role of Special Education Needs Coordinators (SENCOs) in this process. Lorraine Petersen is well-positioned to contribute to this discussion; as former CEO of the National Association of Special Needs (nasen), she has many years' experience of working with pupils with an array of special and additional needs and the teachers, SENCOs and support staff who work with them. No less vital is the importance of engaging families and communities in the transition process, which Claire Wilkinson explores in Chapter 7 by drawing upon her own doctoral work examining parental perceptions of the importance of their engagement in their child's secondary education and offering a comparison between UK-born and immigrant parents.

Chapter 8 considers behaviour and integration into school culture, illuminated by Karl Rogerson's work with the Education Endowment Foundation and as the headteacher of a research school. Many children, families and school staff can find the changes in behaviour and cultures between primary and secondary education difficult to navigate and prepare for, and Karl offers a wealth of practical suggestions to help support this process. Researcher Charlotte Bagnall draws upon her own extensive research in Chapter 9 to examine pastoral matters and emotional wellbeing in schools, and discusses the need to support children's emotional wellbeing over primary–secondary school transitions. Finally, Elizabeth Gregory looks at the impact that disadvantage can have on transitions across the education life course, with a particular focus on poverty and the need for school staff to know what that looks like in their own local area.

We hope you find the book both practical and inspiring, and that you enjoy reading the contributions from our chapter authors just as much as we did.

Part 1

Academic Curriculum

1

Transition into Early Years

Mandy Pierlejewski and Jennifer Holly

Overview of chapter

This chapter examines transition into early years settings, specifically focusing on transition into school-based early years classes. It is authored by two former early years teachers who are now teacher educators in England. It draws upon recent relevant research as well as extensive experience of teaching early years children.

The chapter begins with an overview of current policy in school-based Early Years Foundation Stage (EYFS) provision. This section outlines the broad scope of EYFS provision in England along with the statutory guidance that governs this provision. The following section looks at the curriculum for EYFS, outlining challenges which this curriculum poses such as the schoolification, or making more school-like, of reception classes and the requirement to teach systematic synthetic phonics (SSP) using government-validated schemes. A discussion of the social and relational challenges to transition follows, which focuses on the importance of the key person and the limitations within practice to this approach. Assessment within the EYFS is the focus of a subsequent section, outlining both the formal and informal assessments which take place within the EYFS. This is followed by an evaluation of the impact of place on transition, focusing on the importance of community partnerships. Discussions of the impact on both teachers and leaders complete the chapter examining the specific challenges faced by groups of children and the role of the practitioner in supporting their transitions.

Current policy in school-based EYFS in England

Transition into an early years setting in England can occur at a variety of ages, and for some children can involve repeated transitions as they develop and move settings. The English early years system is made up of a combination of settings, ranging from childminders, through voluntary and private nurseries, and culminating, for most 4–5-year-olds, in a period in a reception class in a school. Transition in the early years can therefore be taken to mean transition into an out-of-home Early Care and Education (ECE) institution (when a child first attends any type of non-family care and education), transition into a school-based ECE institution (school nursery or reception class) or transition between ECE settings, with some children attending more than one setting across the week (a mix of childminder and school nursery, or two nursery settings for example). In addition, children attending a setting will experience transitions through the day, as the needs of routines, staffing and children naturally demand. This can include separating from their main carer at the start of the ECE day, movement between rooms within the setting, changes of activity and so on.

For the purposes of this chapter, we will focus on transitions *into* school-based EYFS settings which include both school-based nursery provision for 3–4-year-olds and reception classes. For these, what is common are the curriculum structure and the availability of places in a reception class. Children may attend nursery part- or full-time before generally moving to full-time attendance in reception classes. All settings *must* follow the EYFS Statutory Framework (Department for Education, 2023c). Prior to reception class, parental choice in the type of setting a child attends is allowed up until the child reaches the compulsory school starting age (Department for Education, 2024a). Government statistics in 2023 revealed that 94 per cent of all 3- and 4-year-olds eligible for a funded place were accessing one indicating that this is a stage of care and education experienced by almost all young children in England (Early Years Statistics Team, 2023b).

Managing academic changes and curriculum requirements

This section will explore the curriculum and academic expectations of the EYFS, identifying aspects that prove challenging for transition such as the schoolification of reception. The early years phase, which can be defined in England as from birth to five years old, is governed and regulated by the EYFS Statutory Framework with separate guidance for groups and childminders (Department for Education, 2023d; Department for Education, 2023e). These documents set out the standards for learning, development and care, including expectations for educational outcomes at the end of the phase as well as regulations for the care of young children in a variety of settings. When a framework for the education and care of children from birth to five years was first introduced in 2008 (Department of Children Schools and Families, 2008), it was intended that such a comprehensive document would ensure a smooth transition from one setting to another as all settings would follow the same framework. This, however, has often not been the case as the diversity of settings and reduced format of the more recent framework has led to significant differences in pedagogy and curriculum between settings.

Reception seen as both 'early years' and 'school'

The pedagogy and curriculum found in reception classes in schools, in which children aged four to five are taught, deviate significantly from the pedagogy and curriculum found in all other ECE settings. In most non-school contexts, learning through play is the dominant pedagogy with staff aiming to achieve a balance between child-initiated and adult-directed play (Palaiologou, 2016). As reception classes are a part of schools however, they can be seen as requiring similar approaches to teaching as other classes in the school. Teachers of reception children may not have expertise or training in early years pedagogy as there is no requirement for them to specialize in this area in their initial teacher education. This can result in 'schoolification', a term which the Organization for Economic Co-operation and Development (OECD) use (2006), which describes the process by which expectations and practices traditionally found in primary school contexts are adopted within early years provision.

Formal vs informal teaching and learning

The EYFS Statutory Framework states that 'Children learn through play, by adults modelling, by observing each other and through adult-guided learning' (Department for Education, 2023e, p. 7). Although research into early learning indicates that play is the vehicle through which young children predominantly learn (Broadhead & Burt, 2012; Brock et al., 2019; Wood, 2013), play is mentioned as one of several approaches to learning which the teacher can adopt. The balance of play-based and teacher-directed learning can be determined by the setting, with some schools choosing a more teacher-directed formal approach to learning and others taking a more child-led play-based approach. The role of the child also varies in these different approaches, as the latter approaches give the child more autonomy and independence as they choose which activities they would like to participate in. More formal, teacher-directed approaches demand much more compliance from the child and reduce their independence as they are directed to tasks rather than choosing them (OECD, 2006). The OECD note that this impacts on transition as children who are used to a play-based approach in their previous settings find the transition more difficult as both the level of autonomy and the approach to pedagogy are very different in more formal reception classes.

Systematic synthetic phonics

Practitioners within early years settings can make choices about their curriculum and pedagogy in all areas except one: literacy. The literacy Early Learning Goal (ELG), which is the expectation for the end of EYFS, expects children to learn to read and write using Rose's model of the simple view of reading (Rose, 2006), which consists of language comprehension and word reading. Although there is no mention of this in the EYFS statutory framework, teachers must use SSP as their approach to teaching reading and writing. This is made clear in the Reading Framework (Department for Education, 2023f) which states that when inspecting schools, inspectors from the Office for Standards in Education, Children's Services and Skills (Ofsted) will evaluate whether SSP is taught from the beginning of reception. This is the only approach to teaching reading and writing which is permitted, and schools are also strongly encouraged to choose from a range of government-validated schemes (Department for Education, 2023a). The available SSP schemes teach the subject through direct teaching, with very little focus on contextual or play-based learning. The schemes are based on memory learning, with repetition and didactic approaches at their heart. This impacts on transition as this approach is very different to the play-based, child-led learning which many children will have experienced in their previous settings.

Key takeaways:

- More formal approaches to teaching reception create challenges for transition as the pedagogy can be very different from previous ECE settings.
- Systematic synthetic phonics must be taught using direct teaching, an approach which may be unfamiliar to many children.

Social/relational changes

Another way in which transition may be experienced on entry into school-based ECE in England is in relation to the structure of the setting and relationships found within them. In Private, Voluntary and Independent (PVI) ECE settings only 8.6 per cent of staff held accredited graduate status in 2023 (Early Years Statistics Team, 2023b), meaning very few children attend a setting with a graduate staffing ratio of 1:13. Where accredited graduates are not employed as staff in ECE settings, children must be cared for at ratios of 1:5 (staff:children) for children aged two, and at a ratio of 1:8 for children aged three-years and above. This then jumps to a ratio of 1:30 for children attending a reception class within a school, as per infant class size regulations (Department for Education, 2023e). This means that the level of adult support and interaction children may experience after transition to reception class could be significantly less. The EYFS also indicates that staffing should be arranged to allow all children to have a named key person, and this applies in all types and sizes of settings across the birth to five years age range (Department for Education, 2023e). However, it could be argued that such ratios do not lend themselves effectively to the implementation of the key person approach, as Elfer and colleagues (2011) argue.

The key person approach is one which has been a part of the EYFS since its inception in 2008. Elfer and colleagues (2011) highlight the benefits of such an approach for all individuals involved in the ECE setting. For the children, it creates a relationship of professional attachment, enabling the child to feel loved, protected and cared for when away from their home environment, while for their parents it provides an opportunity for building a cooperative relationship with a person who is committed to and familiar with their child. Elfer and colleagues (2011) also highlight the significant benefits for the staff working as a key person. For the individual staff member, it enables a genuine relationship to be formed in which they can see themselves having an impact on the development and wellbeing of the child, and for the ECE setting this can be translated to staff who feel more valued and valuable, thereby creating a more stable and committed workforce.

The key person approach is underpinned by Bowlby's (1953) attachment theory, which emphasizes the importance of secure attachments to caregivers and Bronfenbrenner's ecological systems theory (1992), which focuses on the communities surrounding the child from the immediate family to the wider national context. Conkbayir and Pascal (2014) provide a useful overview of the main influences of theorists on current EYFS practices, highlighting the role of attachment in the key person approach and developing effective working relationships with parents, families and communities. Key amongst these is that the child is a part of a community that shapes them and that when teachers work with that community children's outcomes are supported and improved. However, as Elfer and colleagues (2011) highlight, expecting a single teacher of thirty children in a reception class to carry out the role of the key person to each child will likely dilute and limit the impact of this.

We have both experienced this approach to being the key person within school-based reception classes, and the limited opportunity to build genuine and effective relationships with the children and their families. This is not to say it is true of all the relationships forged within the classroom, but often those children and families who most need professionally caring relationships with the school community they are entering will be those least likely to develop them when the key person is so stretched. As Elfer and colleagues (2011, p. 92) state, 'Welcome packs and parents' evenings cannot take the place of a personal relationship of trust between a particular member of staff and a child and a family.'

Key takeaways:

- The quality of relationships in ECE settings can positively influence the development of children, as well as the wellbeing and motivation of staff (Elfer et al., 2011).
- Supporting the child to develop within a community can have positive impacts on development and relationships.
- Staff:child ratios can negatively impact such relationships and therefore put children's development at risk.

Assessment

Teachers and practitioners working in EYFS conduct a wide range of both formal and informal assessments, many of which support transition from one EYFS setting to another. This section will explore both forms of assessment, from informal approaches such as observations, home visits and home-school digital assessment systems to formal statutory assessments such as the two-year progress check, reception baseline assessment and the EYFS Profile. The EYFS Statutory Framework outlines the requirements for both forms of assessment, emphasizing the importance of formative or 'ongoing assessment' (Department for Education, 2023e, p. 19) as well as details about the administration of the three statutory assessments.

Informal assessment

The EYFS Statutory Framework describes ongoing assessment as 'an integral part of the learning and development process' (Department for Education, 2023e, p. 19). Assessment is integral because it enables practitioners to know children and plan for their learning and development based on that knowledge. The document stresses the importance of liaising with parents and carers in these 'day-to-day observations', valuing the observations made by parents and carers as well as those made by practitioners. It also specifically notes that practitioner knowledge is preferable to written records (Department for Education, 2024b). There are several forms of assessment which many practitioners use specifically to support transition. These include home visits, visits to previous settings and informal baselining.

It is also important to note that when children make the transition between ECE settings or attend more than one concurrently, there is no requirement on practitioners to share information on assessment. However, many ECE practitioners consider information sharing in these circumstances to be good practice and have established systems for doing so. Such good practice also supports the ideas of Bronfenbrenner's ecological systems theory and promotes the holistic development of the child, which is a key tenet of the curriculum framework.

Home visits

Many settings conduct visits to the child's home prior to transition and a close liaison between parents or carers and the school is recommended in the OECD Starting Strong 2 report (OECD, 2006). The home visit is an opportunity for parents or carers and children to become familiar with the staff as well as for staff to observe and begin to form relationships with the child and their family. Practitioners can observe how the child interacts with others in a familiar environment, how they regulate their emotions, how they communicate with others and what their play interests are. This can also be an opportunity for staff to identify any possible additional needs. All this knowledge is then used to plan for transition.

Visits to previous settings

In addition to home visits, many settings make time to visit the previous EYFS setting to observe the child and discuss their transition needs with practitioners. A strong partnership between ECE settings is recommended by the OECD in their report (2006). An informal visit enables practitioners to identify children's play interests, observe their social and emotional development and their communication and language. Practitioners from the previous setting can share their professional knowledge of the child, which they will have built up over time. This can then be used to plan for the learning and development needs of the child. The opportunity to see the new teacher in a familiar setting also supports transition for the child as they can locate the new practitioner in 'their' place. It allows the child to welcome the practitioner into their familiar world so that when they transition into an unfamiliar place, they have a shared memory with the practitioner of the previous setting.

Informal baselining

Many settings conduct informal baseline assessments of children as they enter a new EYFS location. Practitioners may use non-statutory guidance documents such as Development Matters (Department for Education, 2023b) or Birth to Five Matters (Early Years Coalition, 2021) to create their own baseline assessments and may keep a record of these to evaluate progress later on in the year. Baseline assessments can be very useful in establishing the child's current level of knowledge and development. They can be used to plan activities to support learning and development.

Formal assessments

There are three formal assessments which are conducted during the EYFS phase. These are the progress check at age two, the Reception Baseline Assessment (RBA) and the EYFS profile (EYFSP). Below is a brief outline of each of these assessments and how they relate to transition below.

Progress check at age two

This is an assessment of a child's progress in the prime areas which is conducted between the ages of two and three (Department for Education, 2022). Whilst a statutory assessment, it does not directly feed into transition into school so we will not explore this further here.

Reception Baseline Assessment

The RBA is an assessment, introduced in 2021, which is conducted by practitioners within the first six weeks in reception. It assesses children's development in mathematics, literacy, and communication and language. It takes the form of a digital assessment using a digital device, which the practitioner completes along with practical activities and questions for the child (Department for Education, 2023e). The Department for Education plans to make this an entirely digital assessment in 2025, with both the child and teacher using a tablet to complete the assessment (Standards and Testing Agency, 2024) rather than just the teacher working on a digital device, as is currently the case. This assessment is not intended to be used for any form of transition. The Statutory Framework states that the purpose of the RBA is to provide progress data for the primary phase: 'it is solely intended for use within the primary school progress measure' (Department for Education, 2023e, p. 45). However, many teachers use the RBA informally to baseline children, keeping an unofficial record of answers. In this way, the RBA, although not intended to be used for transition, is in fact often used as a facet of transition.

Early Years Foundation Stage profile

This assessment is carried out in June of the reception year and requires practitioners to measure children against the Early Learning Goals (ELGs) for all areas of learning. It is based on practitioners' professional knowledge and requires a best fit judgement as to whether a child has or has not met the ELGs (Department for Education, 2023e). The purpose of this assessment is to inform parents and carers as well as other practitioners and teachers about the learning and development of the child. It aims to give a 'well rounded picture' of the child (p. 21). Data from the EYFSP is also used to measure the 'Good Level of Development' (GLD) (Early Years Statistics Team, 2023a). Data recording children who achieved the ELGs for maths, literacy, communication and language, physical development, and personal, social and emotional development is collated both nationally and locally as well as being used by the school as a key progress indicator. It is a high-stakes assessment as it is used to judge the quality of education in reception classes.

> **Key takeaways:**
>
> - Informal assessments in EYFS are used to support transition.
> - Home and previous setting visits can support practitioners to ensure a smooth transition for children.
> - Formal assessments can also be used to support transition, with the exception of the Reception Baseline Assessment.

Impact of place

School-based EYFS provision takes place within primary schools. Most children will attend primary schools which are within their locality and reflect their local community. The types of school which a child attends can also have an impact on transition. Children may attend a local authority school; a stand-alone academy; a member of a multi academy trust (MAT); an independent school; a free school or a faith school. Schools can be of very different sizes with some having fewer than one class per year and others having several classes in each year. One of the most important factors in any of these schools, however, is the relationship between the school and the community. If a school understands its community, it can adapt its approach to education to best meet those needs. This demands intercultural understanding, where the cultures of both the school and the community develop an understanding of each other (Pierlejewski & Vamosi, 2021). This can impact on transition as families will develop an understanding of the expectations of the school which will be communicated to children. Concomitantly, the school will develop an understanding of the community and will tailor its provision towards that specific group of people.

Intercultural understanding can be a challenge for schools which are part of large MATs. Baxter and Cornforth (2021) explore the challenges of MATs engaging with their community, explaining that governance within a MAT is very different to a stand-alone school. When a school joins a MAT, its governance moves from being school level to multi-level with a board of trustees governing the MAT and a governing board for each school. This has an impact on engagement with the community as many decisions are made at the MAT level without the involvement of the community. A report into MATs found parents felt disconnected from the governance of their schools and MATs were not sufficiently involved with the local community (Parliament UK,

2017). This is understandable as academies within a trust may be spread over a large geographical area and include schools with very diverse communities. As MATs often desire a consistent approach across their schools, decisions about pedagogy, including transition arrangements may be made at the MAT level with little consideration for the local needs of each school.

An Irish study by Tobin and colleagues (2022) explored family–school connectivity during transition into primary school. Although this study took place in Ireland, the process is relevant to English settings as it is similar to many English school contexts. Here, the focus of transition was on developing a partnership with families in the education of their children. Parents were welcomed into the school, and this enabled them to understand the new structures and routines as well as the approach to education. It also enabled the school to understand the families and by extension, the community. This model of working in partnership with the community to support transitions into school depends on an understanding of the local context and enables a more bespoke approach to transition which meets the needs of children.

This research supports the ecological systems theory of Bronfenbrenner (1992) and its influence on children's development. In contrast, where schools do not take a collaborative approach towards transition into the school community, children and their wider families can feel isolated and excluded.

Key takeaways:

- It is important for schools to tailor their transition processes to the local community.
- Intercultural understanding enables the school and community to understand each other.
- Assessment of children's learning and development when transitioning from one setting to another is essential for planning a smooth transition process.

Implications for teachers

For some children, the transition into EYFS is particularly challenging. Groups of children for whom this might be the case are children who have not experienced any kind of early childhood education and care before, children who are in the early stages of learning English; refugees and asylum seekers and children from cultural backgrounds which differ from the dominant culture of the setting.

Identifying transition needs

Prior to starting in the new ECE provision, practitioners need to identify those children who may struggle with transition. This can be done through communication with parents and carers or previous settings. An assessment that takes place within the home visit is an ideal basis from which to identify possible needs. Some settings also use audits providing a structured approach to the identification of possible challenges. An example of a useful audit can be found on the Transition for All into School website (Trains Research, 2022). These can be helpful in creating a hierarchy of needs, which practitioners can then use to plan additional support where appropriate. Children with multiple challenges, such as those with special educational needs *and* English as an additional language, may well have higher transition needs than some with only one challenge. From the needs audit, a smooth transition can be planned.

Supporting children who have not been to a previous ECE setting

For children who have been cared for by family members prior to starting in a setting, transitioning from home care to out-of-home care can be a significant change. They may have very little experience of leaving their main carers or being with a group of other children. The people, structure and location of the new ECE setting will all be completely new for such children. To ensure a smooth transition, a gradual integration approach can be very helpful, involving children attending the new setting with their parents for regular visits and stay and play sessions. When the child has become acclimatized to the new environment, the parent or carer can begin to leave the child for very short periods of time. These periods would increase until the child settles for the whole session. This integration period may differ and should be designed for the specific child, rather than adhering to a set timeframe.

Supporting emergent bilinguals

Children who are in the early stages of learning English can find transition difficult because communication with the staff team and other children can be limited. They may also belong to communities whose values and beliefs differ from those of the school, which can also prove to be a challenge for transition as the new setting is culturally unfamiliar. A strategy which can help young bilinguals is to buddy them up with a child who speaks the same language. This can encourage communication in the home language, giving the new child an opportunity to develop peer relationships. Another strategy is to involve cultural liaison workers. These may be parents or community members from the same language community as the child and who can use home language in the setting. Cultural liaison workers can also be invaluable in communicating with families who may also struggle to speak to staff in English. This approach was used with Roma Gypsy children in an ECE setting in England. The cultural liaison person was able to translate both culture and language from the community to the school and from the school to the community, thus promoting intercultural understanding (Pierlejewski & Vamosi, 2021).

Supporting children who are refugees and asylum seekers

For those who have recently entered the country seeking asylum or as refugees, there are multiple challenges to transition. Such children may have experienced trauma, which can impact on them in different ways. They may be easily triggered to relive the trauma, may be in the early stages of processing the trauma and may struggle to trust staff. They may also have language barriers and cultural differences which also make transition more complicated for some. An approach that can support refugee and asylum seeker children found in the TRAINS resources (Trains Research, 2022) is to focus on educating staff about the incoming families. Staff can be trained in supporting children with PTSD and trauma, the situation in the home country, the cultural differences and language of the home country and the education system of the home country. Adjustments can then be made to ensure that changes are kept to a minimum. Small things like providing food that is familiar to the children can minimize the shock of transitioning into the new setting.

Supporting children with special educational needs and disabilities

For some children with special educational needs and disabilities, transition can be particularly challenging as the level and nature of the support they are already receiving may change. For such children, multi-agency working is essential, requiring effective partnerships with other professionals such as medical professionals, speech and language support, specialist educators, social workers and the parents or carers of the child. For those who need it, a transition plan is useful, formulated in partnership with the various agencies working with the family.

Supporting children who have been to a previous ECE setting

For children who have previously attended an ECE setting before coming into the school environment, the transition can also be significant. Many of the commonly used transition practices, such as staggered starts and half-day attendance in the first weeks of the school year can be significantly disruptive to the routines already established in the family where the child has been in full-time nursery. This change from full days of out-of-home care, to a patchwork of part-time school attendance and family or other ECE setting care can often leave the child confused about the nature of school, especially when they have been built up to expect they are moving onto something exciting and only for 'big children'. These additional stressors placed on the family can also colour the perception of school held by the parents, who may need to use annual leave, parental leave or call on other family members to support.

Key takeaway:

- Auditing and understanding transition needs are essential for supporting those for whom transition may be challenging.

Implications for leadership

For school leaders with a focus on the leadership, management and organization of the whole school, some of the detail of transition into school can seem trivial, and focus can be easily lost. For anyone already working within a system, regardless of their level or age, it is all too easy to overlook how different that system might be for anyone entering it from outside, even if they have had similar experiences previously. However, research has shown that ensuring parents are confident with the care and support their children are receiving means they are more likely to be supportive of the system delivering this support. Desforges and Abouchaar (2003) work alongside the research findings of the Effective Provision of Pre-school Education (EPPE) project (Sylva et al.,

2004) informed the EYFS theme of Positive Relationships, promoting the need for ECE to be a collaboration between the setting and the family. Rather than making the building of this relationship one-directional (schools informing parents) the research highlights the importance of the knowledge of the families, in much the same way as the research discussed in the 'Impact of Place' section above does.

Therefore, school leadership needs to empower the staff working with the child and their family on transition, to offer individualized approaches. This will likely involve consideration of time, staffing, flexibility of attendance and attitudes towards parents being physically in the school. An understanding needs to be established that the school needs to support both the child *and* their family in the transition, and that transition is not a one-off event. As the year progresses children and their families can become more used to working within the structures of the school, but nursery and reception classes should be seen as an opportunity to operate outside of these constraints to provide a strong and effective start to formal schooling.

Further reading and support

Useful information about transition into EYFS settings can be found in the following sources:

Early Years Coalition (2021) *Birth to 5 Matters: Non-Statutory Guidance for the Early Years Foundation Stage* [Online]. St Albans: Early Education. Available from: www.birthto5matters.org.uk.

Elfer, P., Goldschmied, E., & Selleck, D. (2011) *Key Persons in the Early Years : Building Relationships for Quality Provision in Early Years Settings and Primary Schools*. Oxford: Taylor and Francis Group.

OECD (2006) *Starting Strong II: Early Childhood Education and Care* [Online]. OECD Publishing. Available from: http://www.oecd-ilibrary.org/education/starting-strong-ii_9789264035461-en [Accessed 6 July 2017].

Trains Research (2022) *Transition for All into School* [Online]. Transition for All into School. Available from: https://eutrainsproject.eu/ [Accessed 28 June 2024].

References

Baxter, J.E., & Cornforth, C. (2021) Governing collaborations: How boards engage with their communities in multi-academy trusts in England. *Public Management Review*, *23*(4), 567–89.

Bowlby, J. (1953) *Child Care and the Growth of Love*. Harmondsworth: Penguin Books.

Broadhead, P., & Burt, A. (2012) *Understanding Young Children's Learning through Play* [Online]. London: Routledge. Available from: https://doi.org/10.1016/j.solener.2019.02.027%0Ahttps://www.golder.com/insights/block-caving-a-viable-alternative/%0A???.

Brock, A., Jarvis, P., & Olusoga, Y. (2019) *Perspectives on Play: Learning for Life*. Abingdon: Routledge.

Bronfenbrenner, U. (1992) Ecological systems theory. In: Vasta, R. ed., *Six Theories of Child Development: Revised Formulations and Current Issues* (pp. 187–249). London: Jessica Kingsley Publishers.

Conkbayir, M., & Pascal, C. (2014) *Early Childhood Theories and Contemporary Issues : An Introduction*. London: Bloomsbury Publishing Plc.

Department for Education (2022) *Progress Check at Age Two*. Forest Row: Crown.

Department for Education (2023a) Choosing a phonics teaching programme [Online]. *Department of Education*. Available from: https://www.gov.uk/government/publications/choosing-a-phonics-teaching-programme/list-of-phonics-teaching-programmes [Accessed 14 June 2024].

Department for Education (2023b) *Development Matters*. Forest Row: Crown.

Department for Education (2023c) *Early Years Foundation Stage (EYFS) Guidance on Exemptions*. London: Crown.

Department for Education (2023d) *Early Years Foundation Stage Statutory Framework for Childminders*. London: Crown.

Department for Education (2023e) *Early Years Foundation Stage Statutory Framework for Groups and School-Based Providers*. London: Crown.

Department for Education (2023f) *The Reading Framework*. London: Crown.

Department for Education (2024a) School admissions [Online]. *GOV.UK*. Available from: https://www.gov.uk/schools-admissions/school-starting-age#:~:text=Your child must start full,school age on that date [Accessed 28 June 2024].

Department for Education (2024b) Reducing paperwork [Online]. *GOV.UK*. Available from: https://help-for-early-years-providers.education.gov.uk/support-for-practitioners/reducing-paperwork [Accessed 20 February 2025].

Department of Children Schools and Families (2008) *Statutory Framework for the Early Years Foundation Stage: Setting the Standards for Learning, Development and Care for Children from Birth to Five*. Nottingham: DCSF Publications.

Desforges, C. & Abouchaar, A. (2003) *The Impact of Parental Involvement, Parental Support and Family Education on Pupil Achievements and Adjustment: A Literature Review*. Volume 10. Nottingham: DfES Publications.

Early Years Coalition (2021) *Birth to 5 Matters: Non-Statutory Guidance for the Early Years Foundation Stage* [Online]. St Albans: Early Education. Available from: www.birthto5matters.org.uk.

Early Years Statistics Team (2023a) Early years foundation stage profile results [Online]. *GOV.UK*. Available from: https://explore-education-statistics.service.gov.uk/find-statistics/early-years-foundation-stage-profile-results.

Early Years Statistics Team (2023b) Education provision: Children under 5 years of age [Online]. *GOV.UK*. Available from: https://explore-education-statistics.service.gov.uk/find-statistics/education-provision-children-under-5 [Accessed 28 June 2024].

Elfer, P., Goldschmied, E., & Selleck, D. (2011) *Key Persons in the Early Years: Building Relationships for Quality Provision in Early Years Settings and Primary Schools*. Oxford: Taylor and Francis Group.

OECD (2006) Starting strong II: Early childhood education and care [Online]. *OECD Publishing*. Available from: http://www.oecd-ilibrary.org/education/starting-strong-ii_9789264035461-en [Accessed 6 July 2017].

Palaiologou, I. (2016) *The Early Years Foundation Stage: Theory and Practice*. 3rd ed. London: Sage Publications.

Parliament UK (2017) *Multi-Academy Trusts: Seventh Report of Session 2016–17*. Edited by House of Commons Education Committee. London: UK Parliament. Available from: https://dera.ioe.ac.uk/id/eprint/28765 [Accessed 11 April 2024].

Pierlejewski, M., & Vamosi, G. (2021) A Romani analysis of English preschool education. In: Kinard, T., & Cannella, G.S. eds., *Childhoods in More Just Worlds: An International Handbook* (pp. 39–53). Gorham, ME: Myers Education Press.

Rose, J. (2006) *Independent Review of the Teaching of Early Reading Final Report*. Independent review [Online]. March. Available from: www.standards.dcsf.gov.uk/phonics/report.pdf.

Standards and Testing Agency (2024) 2025 reception baseline assessment: IT guidance [Online]. *Gov.UK*. Available from: https://www.gov.uk/guidance/2024-reception-baseline-assessment-it-guidance [Accessed 11 April 2024].

Sylva, K., Melhuish, E., Sammons, P. & Siraj-Blatchford, I. (2004) The Effective Provision of Pre-School Education (EPPE) Project Technical Paper 12: The Final Report-Effective Pre-School Education. DfES and Institute of Education.

Tobin, E., Sloan, S., Symonds, J., Devine, D., Tobin, E., Sloan, S., Symonds, J., Devine, D., Sloan, S., & Symonds, J. (2022) Family – School connectivity during transition to primary school. *Educational Research* [Online], 64(3), 277–94. Available from: https://doi.org/10.1080/00131881.2022.2054451.

Trains Research (2022) Transition for all into school [Online]. *Transition for All into School*. Available from: https://eutrainsproject.eu/ [Accessed 28 June 2024].

Wood, E.A. (2013) *Play, Learning and the Early Childhood Curriculum*. 3rd ed. London: Sage Publications.

2

Transitions to Primary

Liz Stevenson

Overview of chapter

This chapter will focus on the move from Early Years Foundation Stage (EYFS) to Key Stage 1 in England. Throughout I will be focusing on Nursery and Reception classes in the EYFS phase and Year 1 in Key Stage 1. To fully appreciate and support the nuances of this move, I will consider the involvement of parents, the 'receiving' schools and any Private, Voluntary or Independent (PVI) settings. The complexity of the move to the primary phase is huge and the impact of the pastoral, curricular and pedagogical effect should be considered. This chapter will explore ways in which schools can prepare both themselves and families for this change, and will consider early childhood and education research. It has been written with support from current practitioners focusing on EYFS and KS1 learning. There are a range of journeys that children take from EYFS provision to statutory schooling in Year 1, although the bulk of the chapter will focus on those pupils who move directly from reception class to Year 1 in the same setting. This chapter will explore the differences that the children have experienced and how staff from all settings both before and after the transition period can best support the children.

Current policy and context

In England, it is statutory that a child must start full-time education once they reach compulsory school age. This requirement is when a child turns five, but there are three distinct time points that can affect when they begin their education, as detailed on the UK government's website (Department for Education, School Admissions undated) for school admissions. These time points align with the term immediately following the child's fifth birthday:

Pupil turning 5 …

- after 31 December will start school in Spring term
- after 31 March will start school in Summer term
- after 31 August will start school in Autumn term

To put this into context, here are some examples.

- Sian turns five on 20 December; therefore, she must start school in January and will join reception.
- Viktoria turns five on 5 February; she must start school in March/April at the start of the Spring term and will join reception.
- Rakesh turns five on 5 June; thus, he must start school in September and will begin in Year 1.

It is essential to remember that this regulation relates to the start of statutory education. In England, this is divided into four Key Stages.

- Key Stage 1 relates to Years 1 and 2 (ages 5–7)
- Key Stage 2 consists of Years 3–6 (ages 7–11)
- Key Stage 3 refers to Years 7 to 9 (ages 11–14)
- Key Stage 4 is Years 10 and 11 (ages 14–16).

However, children can be part of the school system from the age of three or four, usually through a school nursery or PVI. These early years are governed by specific standards and frameworks designed to support and prepare young children for the transition into Year 1.

The EYFS statutory framework sets the standards that all early years providers must meet to ensure that children learn and develop while being kept healthy and safe. The EYFS promotes teaching and learning to ensure children's 'school readiness'. It provides children with a broad range of knowledge and skills, establishing the right foundation for good future progress through school and life. This framework is pivotal as it addresses both educational and developmental milestones that young children must achieve to be seen as 'ready for school'.

Thought: Does school readiness mean that the child is ready for school or that the school is ready for the child?

The concept of 'school readiness' can be interpreted in two ways: it could mean that the child is prepared and equipped with the necessary skills to start school, or it could mean that the school is adequately prepared to meet the needs of incoming children. Both interpretations highlight the importance of a supportive transition from early years settings to Year 1.

The transition from Early Years Education occurs in a range of settings, which includes nurseries, childminders and reception classes in schools. To facilitate this transition smoothly, statutory guidance needs to be considered. Two crucial documents in this regard are:

- The EYFS statutory framework: Outlines specific areas of learning and development, assessment requirements, and the importance of safeguarding and welfare.
- Development Matters: This is non-statutory curriculum guidance for EYFS. It provides detailed guidelines on how practitioners can support children's learning and development. This document helps educators understand what children need to learn at different stages and offers practical advice on how to implement this in various early years settings.

Both documents are signposted in the 'Further reading section.

Teachers and leaders in school settings need to have at least an awareness of this framework and guidance, as it directly impacts the children's educational journey. In the following section I will consider all areas of the journey that are supported by these guidelines and will break down the documentation into manageable chunks. Suggestions on how to ensure staff in schools are aware of these guidelines will also be provided.

To ensure that staff in schools are well-informed about the EYFS and Development Matters, there are several strategies that can be used. These include:

- regular training sessions
- workshops
- collaborative planning meetings where early years practitioners can share their expertise with primary school teachers
- creating resource materials and providing access to online platforms where these documents can be easily accessed and referenced can support staff.

Understanding and implementing the EYFS statutory framework and Development Matters are crucial for ensuring a smooth transition for children from early years settings to school. This approach helps maintain continuity in children's learning and development and supports the idea that both the child and the school are ready for this significant transition milestone.

By comprehensively preparing both educators and children, the educational journey from birth to the statutory school age of five can be made seamless and effective. This preparation ensures that children are not only academically ready but also socially and emotionally equipped to manage the new environment, routines and expectations that come with starting school.

Key takeaways:

- The EYFS and Development Matters play a critical role in preparing children for school.
- Starting full-time education at the compulsory school age in England is a clearly structured, phased approach based on a child's date of birth.

Academic changes/curriculum

This section will explore the differences between the EYFS framework, particularly the ELGs, and the Key Stage 1 (KS1) National Curriculum. In England this curriculum comprises a programme of study for a broad range of subjects with the aim of 'providing pupils with an introduction to the essential knowledge they need to be educated citizens' (Department for Education, 2014a, p. 4). It will also examine how each stage needs to prepare for and learn from the other, highlighting the differing organization of the curriculum and the necessary pedagogical approaches.

The EYFS curriculum (DfE, 2023) is built around three Prime Areas of Learning:

1. *Communication and language*
   - Engaging in interactive conversations, focusing attention and listening to both adults and peers. Expanding vocabulary by learning new words and connecting them with familiar ones. This area includes both non-verbal and verbal communication skills, such as making eye contact, taking turns in conversation, expressing emotions, recognizing and isolating sounds, processing language and forming speech sounds.

2. *Personal, social and emotional development*
   - Developing social skills like forming attachments and relationships, sharing, and waiting for one's turn. Building confidence, independence

and resilience. This area also addresses personal care, such as hygiene and toileting, as well as fostering self-awareness.

3. **Physical development**
   - Enhancing coordination and fine motor skills, including hand control, attention and concentration, body awareness, sensory processing, postural control and shoulder stability. Gross motor skills involve activities such as improving spatial awareness, core strength, and the ability to sit, stand, walk, run, jump and roll.

A significant consideration when transitioning from the EYFS to the KS1 National Curriculum is ensuring that children have experienced and mastered these areas of learning. It is crucial to support those who arrive in Year 1 without having fully developed these skills.

When preparing a child for school, it is important to remember that the preparation is not always about assessing his/her academic skills. It is about helping him/her to develop positive self-esteem and confidence. A positive disposition will promote a child's readiness for school.

- **Visiting the new setting or school** plays an important part in dispelling fears of the unknown. Encouraging the child to use a digital or disposable camera on such visits can help to make the environment more familiar for the child. This supports a personalized approach, and the autonomy can be very empowering for the child. The photographs can then be shared by the child and discussed in the security of a familiar setting.

- **Effective communication with parents and carers is crucial**; children may disclose their concerns at home. Staff and parent relationships need to be positive to ensure that this information is shared in order that the appropriate support is offered. Ideally parents and carers should be involved in any planning as they have a wealth of knowledge that professionals can draw on.

When comparing the EYFS and KS1 curriculum, it is important to consider different pedagogical approaches. The EYFS framework emphasizes play-based learning and continuous provision, which contrasts with the more formal structure of the KS1 curriculum. A brief outline is below.

Continuous provision

Continuous provision in the EYFS refers to providing children with an environment where they can choose from a range of activities that are always accessible. This approach supports children in developing independence, decision-making skills and self-regulation. For example, an EYFS classroom might have designated areas for reading, construction, role play and creative activities, allowing children to move freely between them.

Formal approaches

In contrast, the KS1 curriculum is more structured, with defined lessons and specific learning objectives. While still incorporating play and exploration, there is a stronger focus on direct instruction and academic outcomes. For instance, the ELG for People, Culture and Communities encourages children to observe, discuss, and recognize cultural and religious differences through stories and experiences. Meanwhile, KS1 geography emphasizes factual locational knowledge, such as naming continents, oceans and understanding UK geography. Schools often implement a transition curriculum to bridge EYFS's play-based learning with KS1's structure, adapting it based on cohort needs and school ethos towards formal or play-based approaches.

- Basic literacy and numeracy skills.
- The ability to follow instructions and routines.
- Social skills such as sharing, taking turns and working collaboratively.
- Emotional resilience and independence.

These are crucial for setting a strong foundation for further learning.

Key takeaways:

- Ensuring that children have mastered the three areas of learning in the EYFS is crucial for their success in KS1.
- EYFS to the KS1 National Curriculum involves significant changes in curriculum and pedagogical approaches that should be considered when planning the transition for children.
- A well-planned transition curriculum helps children adjust to the new expectations and reduces anxiety about the move to Year 1.

Social/relational changes

As already suggested, the transition from EYFS to KS1 is a significant milestone in a child's educational journey. This shift affects not only the curriculum, but also the social and relational dynamics that children experience. This section will explore staff ratios and support provided during this transition, the move from key workers, the impact on staffing and the changes in relationships for the child. The differences experienced socially can vary depending on whether a pupil is moving into Year 1 from an EYFS provision within the school or PVI setting. Here we will explore some of these changes.

Staff ratios and support provided

In the EYFS, staff ratios are typically higher, ensuring that children receive more individual attention. According to the EYFS statutory framework (DfE, 2014a), the ratio is usually one adult to every eight children for those aged three and four in nursery settings, and one adult to every thirteen children when the group leader holds a relevant level 6 qualification. In reception classes, the ratio can be as low as one adult to every thirty children.

As children transition to Year 1, these ratios decrease, with one teacher typically responsible for the entire class, sometimes supported by a teaching assistant. This change can be challenging for children who have been used to more individualized attention. Therefore, it is essential for schools to ensure adequate support during this period, by retaining additional staff or volunteers to help children adapt to the changes.

The move from key workers

In EYFS, children have a key worker, providing emotional security through a stable, trusted relationship. Moving to Year 1, this system shifts to a single class teacher, which can be a significant adjustment. To ease this, Year 1 teachers should receive training on building strong, trusting relationships quickly. Joint planning sessions between EYFS and Year 1 staff help share information about each child's needs, ensuring a smoother transition, especially when children move from different settings.

Developing social relationships

Children's social experiences vary based on their previous settings. Those moving from an EYFS provision within the same school often find transitions smoother due to familiar peers and surroundings, while children from PVI settings may face greater adjustments. The main difference lies in social dynamics and pre-established relationships. Schools typically support this transition with organized days where children meet new teachers, explore Year 1 classrooms and engage in activities that ease them into the new environment. This phase is crucial for fostering independence and building confidence, as positive relationships boost self-esteem, while negative experiences can hinder social engagement and self-assurance.

Key takeaways:

- The difference in staffing ratios between EYFS and KS1 is significant, and children will need preparation and time to adjust.
- Transition days are a pivotal part of the process to fully support children.

Assessment

Understanding the shift in assessment practices between EYFS and KS1 is crucial for ensuring smooth transitions and effective planning. Here I will explore the differences between the Good Level of Development (GLD) assessments in the EYFS and both the phonics and end-of-key-stage tests, as shown in Table 2.1 below. I will also consider the introduction of reception baselines and their implications for progress measurement.

During the transition between EYFS and KS1, staff must provide an EYFS Profile assessment as set out in the EYFS Profile 2024 handbook (DfE, 2023). At the end of the reception year, teachers must provide Year 1 teachers with a copy

Table 2.1 Differences between GLD assessments in EYFS and phonics/end of key stage tests

GLD	Phonics and End of Key Stage tests
This assessment covers a broad range of areas, including: - communication and language - personal, social and emotional development - physical development - literacy - mathematics	The focus shifts towards more specific academic skills of: - phonics and reading. Historically the children would have been assessed through external examinations (SATS) in - Reading - Maths - Writing However, these are no longer statutory and the use of them differs across school settings.

of each child's EYFS Profile, including a record of the child's outcomes against the seventeen ELGs. For each ELG, the child's performance is categorized as either:

- Meeting 'expected' levels, or
- Not yet reaching expected levels ('emerging').

Teachers may also include a brief commentary on how the child demonstrates the three characteristics of effective learning highlighted earlier. While teachers are not required to produce additional written reports for Year 1 teachers beyond these basic requirements, it is essential that both EYFS and Year 1 teachers have sufficient time to discuss and elaborate on the information presented in the EYFS Profile. This discussion ensures that the Year 1 teacher gains a full and comprehensive understanding of each child's development, which is crucial for planning the Year 1 curriculum to meet all children's needs. Additional information shared between staff in the two phases could be:

- Identified barriers to learning,
- Successful strategies that have helped the child overcome these barriers,
- Details of any specific assessments and provisions in place for children with Special Educational Needs and Disabilities (SEND).

With schools now having the choice to administer end-of-key-stage tests, the impact on children's learning and assessment can vary. Schools may choose to continue using these assessments to monitor progress and identify areas for intervention. Alternatively, they may adopt other methods of assessment. This flexibility can benefit schools by allowing them to tailor their assessment practices to better suit their students. However, it also presents challenges, such as ensuring consistency and comparability of data across different schools. Without a standard testing system, it may be harder to identify progress in children.

The introduction of the RBA in 2021 marked a significant change in how progress is measured from the start of a child's education (Department for Education, 2020). Conducted within the first six weeks of a child starting school, the reception baseline assesses:

- early literacy
- communication
- mathematics
- social skills.

These data provide a starting point from which future progress can be measured. Before moving to primary school, children may undergo various assessments in their early years settings. These assessments can include observational records, learning journals and specific developmental checklists. Sharing this information with primary schools is crucial for transition planning, ensuring that teachers are aware of each child's starting points and learning needs.

The quality of these assessments in aiding transition planning depends on their comprehensiveness and accuracy. High-quality, detailed assessments can provide valuable insights into a child's strengths and areas for development, helping teachers to tailor their instruction and support accordingly. However, if assessments are superficial or inconsistent, their use in transition planning is limited for staff.

It is for this reason that the introduction of reception baselines has been met with mixed reactions. Some educators appreciate the comprehensive nature of the data and its potential to inform teaching and learning (Bradbury, 2021). Others are concerned about the pressure it may place on young children and the risk of teaching to the test (Standards and Testing Agency, 2017). It is crucial for schools to strike a balance, using the baseline data as a tool for supporting learning rather than as an endpoint. This is a common concern in the field of education and assessments at all levels (Simmons and Morris, 2021).

Key takeaways:

- There are significant differences in assessment practice and policy between EYFS and KS1.
- Reception baseline assessment offers a comprehensive measure of early progress so long as it is accurate.

Impact of place

Key stakeholders in any child's educational journey are parents and carers. In my experience of working in schools across all Key Stages, it is evident that engagement between home and schools is usually the strongest in the EYFS, and it tends to dwindle as children progress through school. This shift can significantly impact pupils moving from the EYFS to Year 1, particularly if their parents/carers become disengaged during this critical phase. Family involvement plays a key role in children's academic success and emotional wellbeing. Engaged parents are more likely to support learning at home, communicate with teachers and reinforce the school expectations. However, if this engagement decreases, children may feel less supported and connected to their learning environment, which can hinder their transition and overall academic performance.

Transition tips to share with parents

These tips were shared with EYFS leaders in a Midlands Local Authority as part of an Early Years borough-wide training session delivered by A. Flecher in 2023.

- Invite them to engage with the Transition Process through encouraging them to: Attend transition meetings and events organized by the school to help them understand the new environment and expectations.
- Suggest that they use Stories: Share stories that explore new situations like what the child will experience. Show that the use of open-ended stories can empower children to reason and solve problems independently.
- Help them to acknowledge Relationships: To recognize the importance of the child's relationships with both adults and peers. Having friends in the same class can help children adjust to the new environment.
- Remind them to allow Time to Settle: To understand that children may need time to settle into their new environment. A period of regression is normal, and children may stand and observe before joining in.

The shift from EYFS to Year 1 also involves significant changes in structure, and timetabling for the children. As already highlighted, in EYFS learning is often play-based and thematic, allowing children to explore and learn through activities that interest them. In contrast, Year 1 introduces more discrete teaching of subjects and subject disciplines. This transition can be challenging for children who are accustomed to the more flexible and less structured environment of the EYFS.

When a child moves from a reception class to a Year 1 the environment is also a change for them to acclimatize to. An English Reception classroom typically features a variety of areas designed to support different aspects of early learning and development. Examples are outlined in Table 2.2 below.

Simmons and Morris (2021) suggest additional areas for continuous provision, such as a Yoga Station, which helps children with balance and coordination, and a Cooking Station, promoting independence where children can access ingredients and utensils to create their own recipes (p. 22). Areas such as this would very much rely on the expertise of staff as well as the resources and space available.

Table 2.2 Suggested areas in a classroom

A reading area	• Cosy space with a variety of books. • Comfortable seating like cushions or bean bags. • Often decorated with themes to engage children's interest.
A writing area	• Supplies like paper, pencils, crayons, and markers. • Tools for developing fine motor skills like scissors and glue sticks. • Resources to encourage early writing and mark-making.
A role-play area	• Props and costumes for imaginative play. • Themes such as a home corner, shop or doctor's surgery. • Encourages social skills and language development.
A maths area	• Manipulatives like counting bears, number lines and shape sorters. • Puzzles and games to develop numeracy skills. • Resources for learning about patterns, measurements and basic operations.
A creative area	• Art supplies such as paint, brushes, paper and clay. • Craft materials like glitter, stickers and pipe cleaners. • Opportunities for children to express themselves through art.
A construction area	• Building blocks, Lego and other construction toys. • Space for large-scale construction projects. • Encourages problem-solving and fine motor skills.
An investigation area	• Science resources like magnifying glasses, magnets and natural objects. • Activities that encourage curiosity and exploration. • Tools for simple experiments and observations.
An outdoor area	• Access to a safe, enclosed outdoor space. • Equipment for physical play like climbing frames, tricycles and sandpits. • Opportunities for gardening and exploring nature.

A Year 1 classroom will build on these foundations laid in Reception and will continue to have set areas for development, but it also generally introduces a more structured approach to learning.

> ### Key takeaways:
>
> - It is important to consider the environmental differences that the children will be experiencing during the move from Reception to Year 1.
> - The difference in the formality of each of the settings and the expectations that surround these will be a change that the pupils need to adapt to.

Case studies

Case study 1 is based on one school in the Midlands that I have worked closely with. The school has implemented a comprehensive approach to supporting their children transitioning from Reception to Year 1, ensuring a smooth and positive experience. Recognizing the significance of this change in the children's academic and social development, the school has implemented strategies that focus on continuity, communication and individualized support.

The school has adopted a 'bridging' curriculum that aligns the play-based learning of Reception with the more structured environment of Year 1. During the final term of Reception, teachers gradually introduce elements of the Year 1 curriculum, such as short whole-class lessons and structured activities. Year 1 classrooms are also adapted to include familiar resources and areas that reflect the Reception environment, such as role-play corners and exploration zones in order to provide their children with a sense of continuity between the phases.

The school emphasizes the importance of communication between staff, parents and pupils. Reception and Year 1 teachers work closely, sharing detailed information about each child's learning preferences, progress and social needs. This collaborative approach ensures that Year 1 teachers are well-prepared to support the children's individual needs. Additionally, parents are kept informed through regular meetings and workshops, helping them understand the transition process and how they can support their children at home.

The staff identify children who may find the transition more challenging and provide targeted support. They employ additional teaching assistants who offer one-on-one or small group sessions, focusing on both academic and emotional readiness. For children with SEND, the teachers work closely with the Special Educational Needs Coordinator (SENCO) to develop personalized transition plans.

By integrating these strategies, the staff successfully support children in making a confident and comfortable transition from Reception to Year 1, fostering a positive start to their continued education.

Case Study 2 – from a second Midlands-based school. Child A transitioned from the reception class to Year 1.

Child A is a bright and curious pupil and she moved from EYFS to Year 1 with initial enthusiasm but also with high levels of apprehension. In her reception class, she thrived in a play-based environment, developing strong social skills and a love for storytelling. In the move to Year 1, she found the structured curriculum challenging but with the support of her teacher she quickly adapted by fostering her interests in reading and providing structured activities. This was due to the EYFS staff and the Year 1 teacher holding regular and ongoing discussions about all of the children transitioning and it meant that there was a seamless journey for Child A as well as the other children in her class. The EYFS staff were able to share details of Child A's likes and dislikes as well as strategies of support that had both worked and failed in the past, allowing the Year 1 teacher to provide appropriate support in the early days of the child's time in Year 1.

Implications for teachers

Through Continued Professional Development (CPD) teachers can be better prepared to create inclusive and supportive learning environments that cater to the individual needs of all Year 1 students, regardless of their starting points. If any number of Year 1 students have not met GLD by the end of Reception, it poses a challenge for teachers to effectively meet their needs. Professional development becomes crucial in equipping teachers with strategies and skills to address these challenges. Training sessions focused on differentiated instruction, assessment strategies and targeted interventions can empower teachers to support diverse learners effectively. These can be developed in partnership with experts in both EYFS and KS1 supporting cross-phases collaboration even further. This collaboration with colleagues, including specialists in SEND, can provide valuable insights and strategies.

In a Year 1 classroom there may be limitations with space and the use of this both indoor and outdoor compared to EYFS. Teachers can prepare for these by creatively maximizing available areas for different learning zones. They should assess if the designated room allows for both continuous provision and outdoor activities, ensuring adaptability in planning to optimize learning environments and opportunities as effectively as is possible.

There are several practical strategies that can be employed by teachers and staff in Year 1 to support the induction of pupils into the Year 1 environment from their EYFS provision.

1. **Gradual introduction to KS1 expectations**: Introducing elements of the Year 1 curriculum and routines gradually during the latter part of Reception helps to familiarize the children with new expectations and will therefore reduce any anxieties they may be feeling.
2. **Induction visits**: Organizing transition days or visits where children spend time in their new Year 1 classroom, meet their new teacher, explore new resources and experience the new routines. This helps children feel more comfortable and prepared for the transition.
3. **Supporting emotional wellbeing**: Implementing strategies such as circle time discussions, storytelling and activities focused on emotions and friendships to support children's social and emotional adjustment to Year 1.
4. **Flexible transition period**: Recognizing that children transition at different rates and will have been in their reception class for different periods of time. Offering some flexibility in adapting teaching approaches and providing additional support where needed ensures inclusive practices that support all children.

Transitioning from EYFS to KS1 may present challenges for the pupils and these should be considered carefully by staff. Examples of some of these challenges could be:

- **Academic Expectations**: Adjusting to more formal learning environments and increased academic expectations.
- **Social Adjustment**: Developing new peer relationships and navigating larger class sizes and structured routines.
- **Continuity of Learning**: Ensuring that children's learning progression is seamless and builds upon their prior experiences and achievements in the EYFS.

Implications for leadership

Effective leadership during the transition from EYFS to Year 1 in schools requires careful consideration of a range of factors to ensure a smooth and supportive process for all pupils. Here are key aspects that school leaders need to consider:

Staffing requirements

Leaders must assess staffing needs to support the transition effectively. This involves ensuring that there are sufficient trained and knowledgeable staff members available during transition periods. The allocation of such resources will also mean that there are financial implications for the school and therefore decisions around priorities will be necessary.

Setting requirements – Pupils not ready for primary phase

As discussed earlier, there may be some children who require additional support and reasonable adjustments as they transition from EYFS to Year 1. Leaders promote an inclusive environment where every child's needs are supported to facilitate their smooth transition and ongoing progress.

Pre-transition data/information sharing

Leaders will need to implement secure systems and protocols for exchanging sensitive information while maintaining confidentiality and compliance with data protection regulations. The staffing and the method of this transfer of information should be considered. Access to comprehensive pre-transition data enables Year 1 teachers to tailor their teaching approaches, anticipate support needs and provide targeted interventions from the outset of the academic year.

Planning the school's diary and transition activities

School leaders coordinate the timing and staffing of transition activities to optimize pupil support and readiness for Year 1. They strategically plan transition days, induction visits and joint activities between EYFS and Year 1 to familiarize children with their new environment and routines.

Below are some practical considerations that leaders might want to think about or ask of their staff.

Do you provide opportunities:

- For children and parents to visit Year 1 classrooms and relevant staff well in advance of the move?
- For Year 1 staff to spend time observing children at play, the organization and routines of EYFS classes, EYFS staff supporting child-initiated activities?
- For EYFS practitioners to share the EYFS profiles with Year 1 staff, and explain how the profiles can help establish starting points for each child?
- For children to raise questions, talk about their concerns and to have these feelings acknowledged?
- For children to reflect upon and share their achievements with Year 1 staff?
- For children to talk about how they would like to handle the move and incorporate their suggestions?
- To commemorate their 'graduation' from the EYFS, with, for example, a party, assembly or souvenir book?
- Familiarize yourself with the EYFS guidance and materials supporting transition into Key Stage 1?
- Initially need a modified EYFS curriculum (such as, children who are summer-born, very active or have had a disadvantaged Early Years' experience)?
- Invite parents to an informal session soon after the transition so the children can show off their new class and teacher?

Further reading and support

If you would like to learn more about Continuous Provision and how you can develop this to support transition into Year 1 you can try one of the following:

- https://earlyexcellence.com/latest-news/press-articles/using-continuous-provision/.
- https://early-education.org.uk/continuous-provision-in-eyfs/.
- Simmons, N., & Morris, G. (2021) *Continuous Provision: Creating an Irresistible Early Years Learning Environment.* morrissimmons.com.

If you have an interest in more research-driven and theorist-based guidance for the Early Years, then the following text is a good place to start.

- Bradbury, A., & Swailes, R. (eds.) (2022) *Early Childhood Theories Today*. London: Sage.

Two of the particularly useful government documents that were suggested earlier in the chapter can be found here.

- The Early Years Foundation Stage (EYFS) statutory framework: Department for Education (2014b) Early Years Foundation Stage Framework. Available at: https://www.gov.uk/government/publications/early-years-foundation-stage-framework-2.

Development Matters: This is non-statutory curriculum guidance for EYFS but is useful for practitioners. Department for Education (2017) Development Matters. Available at: https://www.gov.uk/government/publications/development-matters-2.

References

Bradbury, A. (2021) *Early Childhood Theories Today*. London: Sage.
Department for Education (2014a) National curriculum. Available from: https://www.gov.uk/government/collections/national-curriculum.
Department for Education (2014b) Early years foundation stage framework. Available from: https://www.gov.uk/government/publications/early-years-foundation-stage-framework-2.
Department for Education (2017) Development matters. Available from: https://www.gov.uk/government/publications/development-matters-2.
Department for Education (DfE) (2020) *Reception Baseline Assessment: Framework*. London: Department for Education. Available from: https://www.gov.uk/government/publications/reception-baseline-assessment-framework.
Department for Education (2022) Early years foundation stage profile, 2022 handbook.
Department for Education (DfE) (2023) *Statutory Framework for the Early Years Foundation Stage: Setting the Standards for Learning, Development and Care for Children from Birth to Five*. London: Department for Education. Available from: https://www.gov.uk/government/publications/early-years-foundation-stage-framework--2.
Department for Education (undated) Admissions. Available from: https://www.gov.uk/schools-admissions/school-starting-age.
Simmons, N., & Morris, G. (2021) *Continuous Provision: Creating an Irresistible Early Years Learning Environment*. morrissimmons.com.

Standards and Testing Agency (2017) *Early Years Foundation Stage Profile 2018 Handbook*. London: Standards and Testing Agency.

Standards and Testing Agency (2022) *Reception Baseline Assessment Framework*. Available from: https://www.gov.uk/government/publications/reception-baseline-assessment-framework.

3

Transitions to Secondary

Liz Stevenson

Overview of chapter

This chapter will consider the curriculum, assessment and pastoral impact that moving from Key Stage 2 to 3 can have on the children who experience this transitional phase. It will focus on the English Education system. It has been researched over many years in my role as a teacher in primary and secondary schools as well as a transition manager for a local authority in the West Midlands. I will also highlight the ways in which staff can more explicitly take the changes the pupils are going through into consideration when developing transition, induction and early Key Stage 3 lesson planning and delivery. I will discuss some initiatives that can support the development of a more seamless curriculum between the two phases and how the assessments can have the biggest impact on pupils as they transition between phases. The chapter will also include elements of support that can best prepare the pupils while in Key Stage 2 and how early preparation for the pupils plays an integral part in successful transitions. The move from primary to secondary school is a complex and challenging time in a child's life and there are many factors that should be considered when trying to make this as painless and trouble free as possible for the pupils.

Current policy/context in England

As explained in an earlier chapter, in England, the curriculum is separated into four Key Stages.

In some secondary schools they condense Key Stage 3 into two years and extend the curriculum delivery of Key Stage 4 into three.

Other than the National Curriculum spanning across these four Key Stages, there is currently no centralized policy or government guidance focusing solely on the transfer of pupils between Key Stages 2 and 3. The only exception is for pupils with Special Educational Needs (SEN); the SEN Code of Practice states that during transition the school the pupil is currently attending should share information with the setting that the child or young person is moving to (DfE, 2015). The information shared must also be agreed with parents.

In 2015 Ofsted published research in the 'Wasted Years' of Key Stage 3 (DfE, 2015). This paper explored factors influencing secondary school transition experiences, highlighting challenges and implications for educational support and policy. It found significant educational and developmental setbacks during the transition from primary to secondary school. The result of this has been the development of more curriculum cohesion in some subjects taught in Years 7, 8 and 9 in preparation for the beginning of Level 2 studies. These consist of qualifications that are equivalent to GCSEs (General Certificate of Secondary Education).

This publication shone a light on the need for stronger leadership of Key Stage 3 and in turn the staffing and management of transition into secondary school. It details how leaders prioritize the pastoral needs of the child over the academic and goes on to recommend that the academic development of the pupils is as a key consideration as their pastoral needs if the transition is to be successful. 'Leaders of successful schools set the right culture for learning that is embraced by their pupils from the outset' (DfE, 2015, p. 4). If, as this document found, leaders do not prioritize Key Stage 3 in schools, does this in turn mean that they do not prioritize the transition of pupils from Key Stage 2 and how far is that a leadership issue across the school? We will consider the leadership of transition later in this chapter.

The Teachers' Standards Review (DfE, 2011b) focused on the areas of reading, writing and maths and, of course, at the time of writing it is already thirteen years out of date. However, the report highlighted some key findings, summarized below, that are still concerns for schools today.

The progression of pupils during Key Stages 2 and 3 can be complex and individualized, with patterns that defy a simple linear model. Students often experience periods of regression or stasis in their attainment levels, especially in reading and writing. The likelihood of making progress varies, with students who made significant progress in one term being less likely to continue that trajectory in the following term. Overall, more progress is observed during Key Stage 2 compared to Key Stage 3, with the most progress occurring in the summer term and the least in the autumn term.

Prior attainment plays a crucial role in future progress. Students who were behind at the previous Key Stage are less likely to catch up, particularly in mathematics, where the gap is most pronounced. However, as students advance, the percentage achieving the expected levels of attainment increases steadily through both Key Stages. Notably, by the end of Year 5, a substantial proportion of pupils have already reached the expected level for Key Stage 2, with continued but slower progress noted in Key Stage 3, particularly among high achievers in reading and writing.

Pupil characteristics also significantly impact progress. Boys tend to progress less than girls, particularly during Key Stage 3, with the largest disparities observed in reading. As we will see in Chapter 10, socioeconomic factors, such as eligibility for Free School Meals (FSM), exacerbate these gaps, with FSM-eligible pupils making less progress, particularly in maths. The attainment gaps for pupils with SEN persist across both Key Stages, with notable differences in maths. Pupils with English as an Additional Language (EAL) tend to make more progress across all subjects, often catching up with their peers who have higher prior attainment (DfE, 2011b).

We continue to find ourselves struggling to successfully manage the transition for all pupils from Key Stage 2 to 3. Of course, not all pupils will have a difficult time transferring between phases, but we must focus on supporting all.

Key takeaways:

- The National Curriculum spans all 4 Key Stages
- There is a range of influences on how successful the transition between Key Stage 2 and 3 will be for pupils.

Academic changes across the curriculum

In England there is a statutory duty for all schools to deliver a broad and balanced curriculum. If you are a Local Authority maintained school, you must follow the National Curriculum and any schools such as Academies or Independent schools must be able to evidence that their curriculum is at least as good as the National one.

Table 3.1 below shows Geography examples identifying links between the pupils' learning. An understanding of these connections is vital to develop a curriculum that is as seamless as possible between the two Key Stages. In her post *Leadership of the Curriculum*, Myatt (2021) suggests that to fully understand and embed a curriculum at Key Stage 3 that is suitable and follows a clear line of progression from Key Stage 2 then teachers from Secondary schools should be provided with time to visit and learn from those teaching in Upper Key Stage 2. Myatt suggests that this will mean a strategic approach to Continued Professional Development time and was, in fact, highlighted in the Wasted Years (DfE, 2015) as an area for development across several schools visited. The report highlighted that 'too many secondary schools did not work effectively with partner primary schools to understand pupils' prior learning and ensure that they built on this during Key Stage 3' (Ofsted, 2015, p. 4).

Table 3.1 below shows the development of learning between Key Stage 2 and Key Stage 3 and how the content is cyclical, with skills and knowledge repeating over time and increasing in complexity. Understandably, however, teachers and leaders of subjects have such a heavy workload that being able to identify knowledge and content links through year groups or phases curriculum can be a challenge. If we are to ensure that we consider workload and cognitive load of our staff, we must find a way to make those links to develop on from the curriculum that the pupils have experienced.

Table 3.1 Curriculum links in geography

Geographical skills and fieldwork KS2	Geographical skills and fieldwork KS3
<ul><li>use maps, atlases, globes and digital/computer mapping to locate countries and describe features studied</li><li>use the 8 points of a compass, 4-and 6-figure grid references, symbols and key (including the use of Ordnance Survey maps) to build their knowledge of the United Kingdom and the wider world</li><li>use fieldwork to observe, measure record and present the human and physical features in the local area using a range of methods, including sketch maps, plans and graphs, and digital technologies</li></ul>	<ul><li>build on their knowledge of globes, maps and atlases, and apply and develop this knowledge routinely in the classroom and in the field</li><li>interpret Ordnance Survey maps in the classroom and the field, including using grid references and scale, topographical and other thematic mapping, and aerial and satellite photographs</li><li>use Geographical Information Systems (GIS) to view, analyse and interpret places and data</li><li>use fieldwork in contrasting locations to collect, analyse and draw conclusions from geographical data, using multiple sources of increasingly complex information</li></ul>

The example above is just a small sample of the geography curriculum. This highlights how the geographical skills and fieldwork at Key Stage 2 and Key Stage 3 are designed to create a seamless progression in students' learning as they move from primary to secondary education.

You can see that at Key Stage 2, students begin by learning foundational skills such as using maps, atlases, globes, and digital mapping tools to locate countries and describe features. They also become familiar with basic navigational tools like the 8-point compass, 4- and 6-figure grid references, and Ordnance Survey maps. Fieldwork at this stage focuses on observing and recording human and physical features in the local area, using tools such as sketch maps, plans, graphs, and digital technologies.

As the pupils progress to Key Stage 3, the curriculum builds on these foundational skills. They deepen their knowledge of globes, maps, and atlases, applying this knowledge more routinely in both classroom settings and fieldwork. The use of Ordnance Survey maps is expanded, with the pupils learning to interpret grid references, scales, and various types of thematic maps, including aerial and satellite imagery. Additionally, Key Stage 3 introduces more advanced tools, such as Geographical Information Systems (GIS), allowing pupils to analyse and interpret data with greater complexity. Fieldwork at this stage involves working in contrasting locations and requires the pupils to collect, analyse and draw conclusions from more complex geographical data, integrating multiple sources of information.

The link between Key Stage 2 and Key Stage 3 ensures that students gradually enhance their geographical skills and fieldwork capabilities.

Although the curriculum itself shows clear links between the expected learning, the delivery and the pedagogical approaches adopted by teachers in the classroom are very different between the two Key Stages. For the most part in primary schools, lessons are taught by one teacher who is therefore a non-specialist in most of the subjects they deliver, while in secondary schools the majority of subjects are taught by those who specialize in that area. Having said this, the demands of the curriculum are not so much that a good teacher can't understand and deliver quality content. As I have shown, the skills and demands increase over time and so although not taught by a specialist the pupils are exposed to the content. Secondary school teachers should be able to trust that the learning has taken place, but this may have been in Years 3 or 4 due to the nature of the curriculum and so pupils may need reminding rather than re-teaching of areas that were learned more than a year ago.

> **Key takeaways:**
>
> - The curriculum is designed to develop skills over time and revisit knowledge.
> - Pupils may have been exposed to the curriculum content more than 1 or 2 years prior to the move to Key Stage 3.

Social and relational changes

Zeedyk et al. (2003) highlighted that transition has long been considered one of the most stressful events in a child's life. As well as all the curriculum and pedagogical approaches mentioned earlier, the pupils will be navigating a whole new social structure and will need to find their place in this. Pupils are moving from an environment that (for most pupils) is a safe place for them, where they know everyone and understand their place in the social systems. Pupils have fed back to me that in their primary school they felt safe, that even if they didn't like something or someone, they felt that they still belonged in the school and knew their place. When they then move to secondary school this psychological safety is lost. Even if they have moved with peers from their school, they are now surrounded by so many new people and that one of the hardest things is to find their place.

Case Study

One pupil (Child A) that I worked with while he was in Year 8 found himself in a very difficult predicament. He had been one of just a few pupils who had transferred from his primary school, although he was confident that most were friends and that they would remain friends. Unfortunately, this was not the case and the 'friends' parted ways in the early days of the new term. This left Child A without a friendship group but more importantly without any understanding about what to do next and how to find new friends. By the time that we were working together in Year 8 he was still struggling to find his place in the school and because of this his behaviour had deteriorated over time. He had joined the school with no behaviour issues but while working together and alongside a member of staff from the pastoral team he was able to identify that he had been 'flitting' between groups of friends and often misbehaved to make an impression.

While the lack of settling into school does not excuse his poor behaviour, it does help explain it. The School Transition and Adjustment Research Study (STARS) (UCL and Cardiff University, n.d.) found that during the transition period from Year 6 through the end of Year 7, losing old friends was consistently in the top 5 concerns that the pupils had. It also suggested that a whole school approach is needed to best support transition, rather than one that relies on a small group of staff such as Heads of Year 7 or the SENCO – see Chapter 6. The support and successful induction of pupils into a secondary school cannot be the sole responsibility of these key members of staff who are named as responsible. Child A had faced barriers through social time as well as lessons and there had been interactions with numerous staff. Each of those members of staff missed the warning signs and chalked up all his misdemeanours to poor behaviour. Although a pupil who, on the surface, seemed confident, Child A did not have a trusted adult that he felt he could confide in and with no peers to lean on for support; his only means of communication was behavioural. A whole school approach to transition and understanding of its challenges may well have helped Child A with early intervention and support.

Key takeaways:

- It is not easy for pupils to find their new place in a new social structure.
- A whole school approach is needed to support transition.

Assessment in England

Key Stage 2 Standard Assessment Tests (SATS) take place in May of Year 6; they are externally marked, and the results are shared with schools in July. They come in the form of scaled scores and raw scores and are usually used to set targets for the pupils for KS4, as they enter Year 7. There are differing professional views on the need or benefits of these assessments but at the time of writing they are a statutory requirement. They have been criticized throughout the profession as causing undue stress and pressure on pupils at the age of just 10 and 11. It is also believed that this puts further pressure on staff as the results of these pupil assessments are used as accountability measures for schools, creating a high-stakes system which could be seen to adversely affect teaching and learning. This is especially evident (in some cases) in those curriculum areas that are not assessed in this way.

Secondary schools receive the Key Stage 2 SATS data on the same day as the primary schools do and so have access to all the externally assessed data for their new cohort before they start their journey in school. Prior to this though, many schools will ask for Teacher Assessments to start to prepare for the new year. Not only do schools have access to the results for English, maths and reading SATS results, they also can use the Question Level Analysis (QLA) and therefore any gaps in concepts at cohort level can be addressed in the early part of their curriculum planning.

Even armed with all this information, some schools or some subjects will choose to ask the pupils to sit baseline assessments in the early days of Year 7. This is understandable for those curriculum areas that are not externally assessed. However, there are some things to consider if a school is going to set these assessments.

- What information are you hoping to gather from the results? More importantly what will you do with that information?
- What curriculum are you basing the tests on? Are you asking them to show what they know based on the KS2 curriculum or looking forward to the KS3? Is your KS3 curriculum moving on from KS2 or worked back from KS4?
- How will it guide you moving forward? More importantly, how will it support the pupil's learning?
- What format will the assessments be in? More importantly, have the pupils ever seen an assessment set in that way before? For example, if you are setting a history 'test' have the pupils ever had to show their understanding of history in that way before? Have they ever actually sat a history test? If this is an alien concept or way of working, will they perform to the best of their ability?
- When are you setting the tests? Are you asking pupils to perform their best while they are still in the early days of the school year and already trying to cope with all the changes (emotional, social and academic) that they are going through?

We saw from the findings in the DfE report (DfE, 2011a) that progress differed between phases for pupils and the assumption that a pupil attaining well in one phase means they will automatically continue to do and vice versa does not always track that way. If a school does decide to use baseline testing as well as the Teacher Assessment information and the SATS results, it would serve them well to triangulate that information but also consider the pastoral needs of the pupils as an added data point. These needs should be shared between staff from each school prior to the transition taking place.

Case study

After the introduction of the new National Curriculum in England in 2013 there was a need for the SATS assessments to reflect the curriculum changes and they were updated in 2016 having given pupils three years of new curriculum learning.

As the transition manager responsible for developing the transition between KS2 and KS3 for all pupils in a local authority, I was asked to share the details and the research around these new assessments with secondary school leaders, with the support of primary school head teachers.

What struck me most were the responses from a maths leader in the room. After spending time looking through the Maths papers that the pupils had sat, and the demands of the new curriculum (that he hadn't looked at previously) he decided that his entire KS3 maths curriculum needed to be revisited. He thought that too much emphasis had been placed on number in the autumn term of Year 7 and that much of what was planned was revisiting skills that had been a bigger part of the KS2 curriculum. He had realized that he could move onto higher level skills at pace, compared to the original plans.

This not only shows how important it is to understand the curriculum that is taught through KS1 and 2 but knowing and using the QLA from the SATS results that all schools have access to. Staff can use this information to inform planning. This can in turn boost the progress of the pupils as the gaps in knowledge can be addressed thanks to evidence of these gaps of misconceptions.

Key takeaways:

- Staff in both Key Stages 2 and 3 have access to the same data when it comes to statutory assessments this can be used during staff discussions.
- Baseline tests in secondary school can be most effective when used alongside the data provided through the Key Stage 2 formal assessments.

Impact of place

It is widely recognized and understood that the move from primary education to secondary is a huge change for pupils as they go from being 'the biggest and baddest' (quote from a Year 7 boy in 2024) to being a much smaller cog in a much bigger wheel. The sheer number of differences that the pupils must face is immense. While all staff try their best to mitigate the change there will inevitably be some areas that we miss or don't even realize will be challenging for the pupils.

There is also a vast difference when we consider the area of the country that pupils are based. Most of the West Midlands, where I have spent my entire career, is well populated, with pupils having a choice of schools to consider when moving between phases. Primary schools can work with up to 10 or 11 secondary schools and conversely, secondary schools can receive pupils from between 40 and 80 primaries. In other areas of the country, including some of the Midlands, there is far less choice, if any at all. Pupils may only have one option of secondary school to move to, taking the element of choice away from the pupils. This can be both a positive and negative situation depending on a pupil's circumstances. We also need to remember the impact that the Middle School system can have on transfer of pupils between the Key Stages. Middle schools usually cater for Years 5 through to 8 or 9 and so pupils experience more transition points. The curriculum requirements still change, and this sometimes comes with the changes in pedagogy and delivery but often the environment would remain the same.

Data from the *Schools, Pupils and Their Characteristics: Report* (DfE, 2019) suggest that the average state-funded primary school has 282 pupils on its roll. However, in contrast the average state-funded secondary school has 965 pupils. The difference in the number of pupils comes with its own challenge. 11- and 12-year-old pupils move from being in a school where almost every other child and adult is known to them, to an environment where they are surrounded by strangers. Even those pupils who move from one school to another with peers are faced with a sea of strange faces. The difference in pupil numbers in the two school systems also create the need for other, more structural changes for the pupils to experience.

During the years that I was a transition manager, I had the privilege of speaking to thousands of pupils about the way they feel about transition between primary and secondary school. Table 3.2 below shows a selection of factors that they identified as affecting them. Further on in the chapter I will share some of the implications these can have on staff and look at ways of overcoming potential challenges.

Table 3.2 Differences between primary and secondary school experiences

Issue	Differences
Buildings	**Primary** – small, often one block. Classrooms named after teachers or year groups. **Secondary** – Usually much bigger, often over more than one floor. Classrooms usually named after location e.g. H23 (Humanities block, 2nd floor, 3rd classroom down).
Number of teachers	**Primary** – one main teacher with occasional support or move for some lessons. **Secondary** – At least one teacher for each subject taught.
Number of lessons	**Primary** – Lessons split through the day, but this is not usually noticeable as generally taught in the same room with one teacher. **Secondary** – My experience in secondary schools has been that the number of lessons taught in any given day ranges from 2 to 7, each taught in different rooms with different staff members.
Expectations	**Primary** – Upper Key Stage 2 and particularly Year 6 pupils are often given quite a lot of responsibility around the school. However, if we really consider the amount of responsibility for themselves, this is far less. Examples include usually taken to school, met by staff, escorted to most activities (to and from playtime, lunch time PE), lunches usually chosen in advance. **Secondary** – Far less responsibility given to them in the way of 'jobs' but the responsibility they are expected to have for themselves is the exact opposite of what they have been used to for the previous 6 years in education.
Environment	**Primary** – Often walls and corridors filled with bright and colourful displays and interactivity. **Secondary** – Some pupils have described secondary school rooms and corridors as being 'like a hospital'. Work may be displayed but this is not usually as bright.

Key takeaways:

- Pupils will experience a number of changes through transition points.
- We need to take time to allow the pupils to adjust to all the new challenges they will be going through.

Implications for teachers

As highlighted earlier on in this chapter, pupils experience a great deal of change during the transition from primary school to secondary. Using some of the differences that have been raised by pupils across Years 6 and 7 through my research in schools, Table 3.3 provides some advice on considerations that can be made when trying to prepare or ease the pupils into their new school and social systems.

Table 3.3 Considerations for schools' preparation

Issue	Considerations in school
Buildings	**Maps of school** – Most secondary schools have maps, but my experience has taught me that the style of the map is not one that the pupils will have encountered before. Consider sharing these across primary and secondary schools so that the pupils can start to understand how to use them but also start to get a feel for the layout of the buildings. **Timetables/Classroom names** – I have found that the complexity of names of classrooms can cause a lot of confusion with pupils. However, this can be cleared up with an explanation as to what the codes mean but also a lot of patience while the pupils find their bearings!
Number of teachers	While this is not something that can be prepared for very easily with actual experience, pupils can be taught/reminded about the nature of humans! We are all very different with different personalities and expectations of behaviours that we will accept. One teacher's joke and acceptable response is another teacher's disrespectful and not acceptable response. We should help the pupils identify the appropriate version of themselves for the adult that they are working with. Equally as the adult we need to understand that the pupils need the opportunity to really get to know you and understand your boundaries. This will take time, especially for those staff who are only met once a week.
Number of lessons	A similar story to that above. The number of lessons each pupil has in a day will correspond with the number of teachers that they see. As well as this they need to navigate their way around a school that is a lot bigger than they are used to and the map they have been given makes no sense. Then, on top of all of that they also need to remember what lessons will take place each day and be prepared for this. This alone is a lot of change. We need to be patient when the pupils first arrive and remember that one or two weeks is not enough to learn all the new details!

Issue	Considerations in school
Expectations	• The expectation that pupils be able to manage themselves can be a relatively easy one to help prepare pupils for. Some quick wins started in primary school: Pupils keep belongings with them all day. Nothing to be left in classrooms if they are not in them. • Provide something simple that the pupils must look after and always keep with them. • Towards the end of Year 6, do not ask the pupils to line up at the end of break/lunch. Expect them to be back in the classroom at the start of the next lesson.

A key difference that I think is sometimes confused by schools is the difference between Transition and Induction. There are two ways of separating the two and deciding which of them is your focus when considering the move from one phase to another.

Transition is person and Induction is place

Transition (between KS2 and KS3) takes time and is spread over several years, preparing the pupils for change and managing the journey through this. We know this takes longer for some than others. Induction is a much shorter period. You are focusing on the physical changes that will be affected by the move from one phase to another: the buildings, the rules, the timetable and so on.

Implications for leadership

In her book *Headstrong*, Dame Sally Coates believes that 'a school is only as good as its Headteacher' (Coates, 2015, p. 235). If this is true, then we must consider whether the quality of the transition into or out of a school is similarly only as good as its leader. While carrying out research for my Masters into the leadership of schools in the UK, specifically using two schools in the West Midlands, I found a contrast between the approaches taken by two schools. The primary school that I was working with regularly reported to the governing body, who are responsible for the overseeing of school business, about transition. They had a policy document in place which was ratified by the board and at the time they were even in the process of allocating the area of transition as a focus for a member of the governing body. In contrast, the secondary school was only occasionally asked to report to governors, and this was more often specifically linked to the cohort of pupils either due to arrive or are already in school. This would have been in the form of a written report rather than attending a meeting, unlike in the primary school where the member of staff was invited to attend.

If schools focus on Transition rather than Induction, then as leaders the decision needs to be made as to when to have the focus on transition in school. The ideal situation would be all year round. Of course, timetable and staffing constraints mean that this would need to be a real culture and policy shift in many schools. Experience has taught me that most of the Induction is confused with Transition and is carried out between March, following notification day in England (for Secondary schools), and after May SATS in England (for primary).

My experience working with schools demonstrates that for a successful strategic approach to transition, leadership at all levels must prioritize it, ensuring it is appropriately staffed and consistently supported. Throughout this chapter I have highlighted the need for not only long-term transition support plans but that this needs to be a whole school consideration.

Key takeaway:

- Transition and Induction cover different periods and can be summed up as: Transition in person and Induction is place.

Further reading

If you are interested in reading that covers both primary and secondary school experiences, then you could consider Dave Harris' book on independent thinking (Harris, D. (2020) *Independent Thinking on Transition*. Carmarthen: Independent Thinking Press).

While both Myatt, M. and Tomsett, J., (2023) *Primary Huh 2: Primary curriculum leadership conversations* (John Catt Educational) and Turner, E., (2022) *Simplicitus Altius: Leading the Interconnected Primary Curriculum* (John Catt Educational) are primary school focused, they both include chapters on transition reflecting both curriculum and pastoral changes.

If you are interested in research papers linked to transition then you could consider a paper led by contributor in this book, Jindal-Snape, D., Hannah, E.F., Cantali, D., Barlow, W., & MacGillivray, S. 2020. A Systematic literature review of primary-secondary transitions: International research.

References

Coates, S. (2015) *Headstrong: 11 Lessons of School Leadership*. Woodbridge: John Catt Educational Ltd.

Department for Education (2011a) *How Do Pupils Progress during Key Stages 2 and 3?* Education Standards Analysis and Research Division. London: Department for Education. Available from: https://www.gov.uk/government/publications/how-do-pupils-progress-during-key-stages-2-and-3.

Department for Education (DfE) (2011b) *Teachers' Standards Review: Research Report DFE-RR096*. London: Department for Education.

Department for Education (2014a) National curriculum. Available from: https://www.gov.uk/government/collections/national-curriculum.

Department for Education (2014b) SEND code of practice: 0 to 25 years. Available from: https://www.gov.uk/government/publications/send-code-of-practice-0-to-25.

Department for Education (2015) Special educational needs and disability code of practice: 0 to 25 years. Available from: https://www.gov.uk/government/publications/send-code-of-practice-0-to-25.

Department for Education (2019) Schools, pupils and their characteristics. Available from: https://www.gov.uk/government/statistics/schools-pupils-and-their-characteristics-january-2019.

Myatt, M. (2021) Leadership of the curriculum. Mary Myatt.com. 27 3. https://www.marymyatt.com/blog/role-of-leaders.

Ofsted (2015) Key stage 3: The wasted years? Available from: https://www.gov.uk/government/publications/key-stage-3-the-wasted-years.

UCL and Cardiff University (n.d.) *School Transition and Adjustment Research Study (STARS)*. London and Cardiff: University College London and Cardiff University.

Zeedyk, M.S., Gallacher, J., Henderson, M., Hope, G., Husband, B., & Lindsay, K. (2003) Negotiating the transition from primary to secondary school: Perceptions of pupils, parents and teachers. *School Psychology International, 24*(1), 67–79.

4

Transitions to Tertiary: Post-16 Education

Elizabeth Gregory

Overview of chapter

This chapter examines transitions in post-16 contexts in England, focusing on tertiary educational providers such as sixth form and further education (FE) colleges, as well as higher education (HE) institutions. Whilst this dual focus means the chapter is broad in scope, a thread runs throughout of perceived inequalities between different educational pathways and providers, and how these affect experiences of moving from one sector to another. The chapter draws on my own experience as a former teacher of A-level English and as a current lecturer in HE, as well as the voices of a number of teachers I have spoken to as research for this chapter. The chapter's case study examines how learners on different educational pathways narrate their experiences of transition from secondary school to post-16 study. Thus, the chapter considers how a learner's choice of qualification or educational institution may affect their experiences of transition, alongside a more general consideration of the challenges and opportunities presented by post-16 transitions.

Current policy in post-16 contexts in England

Whilst this chapter cannot provide a detailed history of the sector, recent key changes relating to transitions are outlined below.

Policy contexts in 16–19 education

In England, perhaps the most significant factor affecting transitions in the 16–19 sector has been raising the school-leaving age from September 2015. All learners must now stay in some form of education or training until 18 (Gov.UK, undated

[a]), rather than being able to leave compulsory education at 16 as previously. Whilst almost all learners in England study GCSEs (a level 2 qualification taken at the end of Key Stage 4) and are limited in the choices they can make, once they enter 16–19 education, more options are available.

In practice, however, these choices are quite restricted. Most learners who choose a level 3 qualification select either a programme of three or four A-Level subjects, or a vocational subject in a single subject (until recently, most likely to be a BTEC, although these were due to be defunded in 2024 and replaced with T-Levels, a similar qualification). Further options include apprenticeships, although the take-up of these in the 16–19 age range is relatively low, and the International Baccalaureate, a level 3 qualification offered by a small number of schools and colleges, largely private. This element of choice can make transitions into 16–19 education both an enormous opportunity and a source of anxiety, as seen later in our case study.

Policy contexts in HE

HE has been heavily impacted by the neoliberal agenda of recent years, which has seen the increasing marketization of the university system. This agenda places the responsibility for HE (and its cost) on the individual rather than society, on the basis that the individual will be the one who benefits from further study.

'Home' students are defined as British or Irish nationals resident in the UK for the three years immediately prior to the start of their course. For these students, tuition fees of up to £1000 per annum were introduced in 1998, then were raised gradually until a fees cap of £9000 per annum was introduced for all HE courses from September 2012 (currently capped at £9250) (Department for Business, Innovation and Skills, 2010). This punitive fee structure means the cost of a university degree is now prohibitive for many, and more students are living at home whilst studying in order to keep costs down – according to a recent survey of 1000 university students, over a third (37 per cent) had chosen to live at home, mostly as a means of saving money (FE News, 2022).

Many UK universities attract significant numbers of overseas students, for whom tuition fees are much higher. In 2021–2 there were 679,970 international students studying in the UK (Universities UK, 2023), including 559,825 from outside the EU, with China providing the highest number of students, followed by India (HESA, 2023). Whilst it is outside the scope of this chapter to explore the experiences of international students, the transition to study in another country presents further challenges and opportunities that will be briefly considered later in the chapter.

> **Key takeaways:**
>
> - School leaving age is now eighteen.
> - Sixteen-year-olds can choose between an 'academic' programme (A-levels, International Baccalaureate) or a 'vocational' one (BTEC, T-level, apprenticeship).
> - The UK attracts high numbers of international students.

Managing academic and curriculum changes

16–19 curriculum and pedagogy

This section considers curriculum, pedagogy and assessment approaches pertinent to A-Level and vocational qualifications. Both pathways are generally taken over two years of full-time study and are classed as Key Stage 5 with content specified by the National Curriculum. Beyond this, the two options share little in common, meaning that the field of 16–19 education lacks the commonality of approach seen across study at Key Stages 1–4.

Studying A-levels

A-Levels (short for Advanced Levels) were introduced in the UK in 1951 and were designed to allow students to develop deeper understanding in fewer subjects. According to consultation documents (Department for Education, 2014), A-Levels help 'students develop the skills and knowledge needed for progression to undergraduate study' (p. 4), suggesting their content and structure are designed specifically as a stepping stone to university.

For learners choosing a sixth form attached to their secondary school, A-level lessons will often be in familiar classrooms with the same teachers who taught them for GCSE. For those transitioning to a separate sixth form college or FE college (see section 5 on Place), teachers and locations will be new, but many familiar aspects will remain, not least in subject choice. Of the most popular subjects studied at A-level, only psychology and sociology are not widely taught at GCSE, so students have some notion of what to expect in terms of content.

However, as A-levels are designed to prepare learners for undergraduate study, they require more independent study than GCSEs. Most learners transitioning to post-16 study are aware of this requirement without really knowing what it is or how to do it, as most of the knowledge needed at GCSE is delivered in class. In the FE college where I used to work, learners received 4.5 hours of teaching per week for each subject, leaving time in their schedules for 'independent study'. Many students saw these as 'free' periods and did not use them for study, and those who wanted to work needed clear direction before they could make good use of their time. Whilst students would complete written homework tasks without issue as they were familiar with this from school, suggestions such as using time to 'read around the subject' were less well understood. These skills need to be modelled in class, such as demonstrating how to use the library search engine to find relevant texts for further reading, and then setting research tasks for learners to complete independently.

Studying BTECs or other vocational qualifications

Vocational qualifications were originally designed to equip learners with skills for a particular job. However, their status is changing, with more than a third of employers valuing vocational and academic qualifications equally (CBI/Pearson; 2015), and more learners entering HE with vocational qualifications than previously (UCAS, 2022).

Learners choosing a vocational pathway are far more likely to face curricular and pedagogical changes than those who have chosen A-levels. Level 3 vocational courses such as BTECs and T-levels are full-time programmes in one single subject, and require regular attendance in a workplace alongside classroom studies. In conversation for this chapter, an experienced Childcare teacher suggested that the biggest challenge for new students is realizing the subject they have chosen is now their sole focus after studying a wide range of subjects at school: 'The thought of doing the same subject all day, every day can be quite daunting, and quite a commitment.' In her experience, this often causes students to question whether they have made the right choice, and – in some cases – change to a different subject or even to an A-level programme offering more variety.

Pedagogically, many classroom-based and homework activities are likely to be familiar from school, although this will vary for different subjects. However, as with A-levels, there is a greater focus on independent learning ('there's far less reliance on a core textbook than in school subjects', commented an FE teacher of Health and Social Care), more flipped learning and a greater requirement to submit work and access resources electronically. One social and pedagogical change specific to vocational courses is the tendency for learners to remain with the same study group all day, rather than moving from one subject to another. The FE teachers I spoke to for this chapter identified this as a strength, citing positive friendship groups as one of the key ways in which learners can successfully manage the transition process.

> ### Key takeaways:
> - Emphasis on independent, in-depth learning, to prepare for HE study.
> - Greater requirement for IT skills and competencies.
> - Many other activities will be similar to those experienced at school.

HE curriculum and pedagogy

My undergraduate days are long gone, but I still remember the shock of being in a huge lecture theatre packed with two hundred students. This was before widespread use of technology, and so we sat, densely packed in tiered rows, feverishly trying to scribble down everything the lecturer said. And as an English Literature undergraduate, I had only eight hours of 'taught' study each week in my first year.

Nothing I had experienced previously come close to preparing me for this. Things have changed for the better in many ways; most HE courses now use blended learning, where online materials and activities are provided as well as face-to-face teaching, and lecturers upload their slides as well as accompanying materials and suggestions for wider reading. To facilitate this, most courses use a virtual learning environment (VLE) platform such as BlackBoard or Canvas, and whilst many schools and colleges also make use of such platforms, it is important not to assume that students have the skills required to successfully access course content.

Most HE learners are also likely to attend regular seminars. These vary greatly in size depending on the course; in my role as HE lecturer, most of my seminars consist of 25–30 students, and thus are closer to the class sizes most learners will already be familiar with. However, the focus on independent learning means that we meet to discuss a particular academic text, or develop ideas delivered in a previous lecture. For students who lack the confidence to critically evaluate a particular reading or concept, the expectation to put forward meaningful contributions in this kind of environment can cause great anxiety.

> **Key takeaways:**
>
> - Independent study skills such as effective use of online library searches become even more crucial.
> - Blended learning often used, with a virtual learning environment used to store and share resources.
> - Learners are not always fully prepared for the expectations of FE/HE, and required skills need to be explicitly taught.

Assessment

Assessment in 16–19 contexts

Revisions to A-Levels in 2015 (Ofqual, 2014) reinforced the message that formal written examinations are the sole true measure of academic capability. In many subjects, coursework was reduced from 40 per cent to 20 per cent of the overall grade, or removed completely. Resits were abolished, giving students one chance to get it right at the end of a qualification they have studied for two years. Whilst students are used to the examination-based focus on GCSEs at school, the stakes at A-level are higher; with only three or four subjects, the prospect of failing one has more significant ramifications.

Most sixth forms and colleges hold formal mock exams at the end of the first year, designed to give learners a chance to practise for the real thing. These mocks can prove rather a shock! A-level examinations are longer than GCSEs (generally 2.5–3 hours rather than 1.5–2 hours), and it is not uncommon to underperform in the very activity designed to boost confidence ahead of the external exams the following summer. Incorporating a range of formative assessments and feedback throughout the year can help prepare students for this high-pressure, high-stakes period.

Unlike A-levels, vocational qualifications are continually assessed through coursework and practical tasks, and often involve a work placement element. This form of ongoing assessment is likely to be new to most learners, as vocational qualifications are structured around a number of 'themed units' that are 'tested throughout the course using assessments based on real-life scenarios' (Pearson; unpaged, undated). For many learners this is a fairer and less-pressurized form of assessment. A recent Pearson survey of BTEC learners found that 76 per cent of respondents chose their course because of the practical, hands-on aspect (Pearson, undated) and the case study discussed later in this chapter also supports this view.

However, ongoing assessment requires organizational and time-management skills. Whilst most students work hard at school, the structure of GCSEs – little or no coursework; exams at the end of the two-year period – means that learners are more used to last-minute cramming than being regularly assessed, and may need help with organizational skills to ease the transition to post-16 study. Similarly, the work placement needs proactive support from teaching staff if the student is to feel confident in the workplace, as this may well be their first experience of such an environment. Something as straightforward as discussing uniform requirements, timekeeping, or the importance of reporting absences can be invaluable.

Assessment in HE contexts

The means of assessment used in HE can often be a reason for selecting the course in the first place – some may be assessed by examination only, by regular written and/or oral assignments, or a combination of the two.

Students are likely to be faced with a broader range of assessment tasks, in genres they have not attempted before. The BSc in Education in which I teach requires students to write traditional essays, contribute to online discussion boards, deliver group and individual presentations, create a podcast, complete work-based portfolios and write a blog – amongst other tasks! As teaching staff, we try to create assignments that challenge students in different ways, but in our bid for variety, we must be mindful that many of these tasks will be new to students, and provide support and guidance accordingly – perhaps some sample assignments, or modelling a suitable structure for a presentation.

We must also remember that students' prior experiences differ. Sometimes this may just be a matter of reassurance or confidence building. A colleague at another institution who teaches a cohort comprising 50 per cent students who entered the course with A-levels and 50 per cent with a BTEC says there is a noticeable difference in confidence when writing particular types of assignment. Students from a vocational background tell her that they do not know how to write an essay; they do, of course, as both BTECs and T-levels require extended pieces of writing using appropriate academic language. Flagging up these kinds of transferrable skills is likely to help students manage the transition to HE with greater success and lower levels of anxiety.

> **Key takeaways:**
>
> - A-levels largely assessed through examinations at the end of the two-year course.
> - Vocational qualifications assessed through a combination of work placements and written assessments.
> - Greater variety of assessment formats in HE.

Managing social and relational changes

Social transitions in 16–19 education

As well as the educational transition to post-16 study, the age-related physical and emotional transition to adulthood can be a tricky one to navigate. At a time of growing independence, a successful educational transition experience can prove additionally important in supporting individuals through changes in their life as well as studies. For some post-16 students, social changes may be minimal; those staying on at their school sixth form are likely to retain a high level of familiarity with both their friendship groups and teaching staff. Those who move to a different institution however, be it a sixth form college or an FE college, undergo significant situational and social change. This may also involve practical matters such as having to travel further, or organizing food for themselves at lunchtime.

One of the key transitional changes, new friendship groups, can be both a source of anxiety and a huge opportunity. Spending five years with the same people can be both a comfort and a restriction – learners are very different people at sixteen when they leave secondary school than the 11-year-olds they were when they started, and transition to post-16 education can offer the chance of a fresh start and even a new identity, as discussed further in this chapter's case study. As well as new friends, transition to college offers potential for different relationships with teachers. When I was teaching A-levels, I encouraged students to call me by my first name, something that many of them found challenging at first; indeed, some continued to call me 'miss' as they felt too uncomfortable to do anything else!

Transition to a sixth form or college also offers more personal and practical freedoms, such as a common room specifically reserved for students to socialize or study in, or no requirement to wear a uniform. For many learners, 16–19 education represents their first experience of being given greater freedoms to come and go with fewer restrictions; an afternoon off-timetable, perhaps, or the freedom to leave school or college premises at lunchtime. This is discussed further in our case study as a means of paving the way for the social transitions required at university.

Social transitions in HE

Many of the challenges and opportunities in HE are similar to those discussed for post-16 – but amplified! For many learners, the university environment offers unprecedented levels of social opportunities, although most will have to navigate this new world with less support from parents and other home networks than during previous transitional periods. For this reason, HE institutions offer both a welcome week to allow new students to meet lecturers and classmates, and a range of clubs and societies to help find friends with shared interests. Most universities also have staff and student social committees, many of these at course level, so that tutors and learners can work together in organizing social activities.

For many students, transition to university involves living in student halls or some other form of shared accommodation. I still remember the shock of sharing a flat (with one bathroom and one kitchen) with seven other girls! Sometimes these experiences can go badly wrong; young people can find themselves forced to share a living space with people with whom they have nothing in common, or who may be inconsiderate to the point of causing mental distress and/or the inability to concentrate on their studies. In these instances, it is vital that the student knows where they can go for help, and that such situations are not acceptable. However, as with post-16 transitions more generally, university offers an opportunity to connect with like-minded people who share the same interests and values, and the school friends the learner thought would be so badly missed are augmented by a new circle of friends.

> ### Key takeaways:
> - New friendship groups and the potential for new interests.
> - Different, more equal relationships with teaching staff.
> - Increasing independence and freedoms over how and where to study and socialize.
> - Old support networks may be weakened, while new ones form in their place.

Impact of place

16–19 education providers

The range of providers available to students transitioning to post-16 may be limited by the qualification they have elected to take. School sixth forms and sixth form colleges tend to offer a narrower provision (generally A-Levels or the International Baccalaureate) whilst FE colleges offer a broader choice of programmes. This division is largely historical; the term 'further education' refers to 'any study after secondary education that's not part of higher education (that is, not taken as part of an undergraduate or graduate degree)' (Gov.UK, undated [b]; unpaged). However, other definitions indicate a more hierarchical separation. The British Council summarizes sixth form colleges as 'specializ[ing] in academic courses to prepare students for higher education' and further education colleges as 'offer[ing] courses and qualifications in a wide range of vocational and academic subjects at many levels' (EducationUK.org; undated, unpaged).

This separation of provision can be reflected in lower entry requirements. For example, the FE college at which I used to work required lower grades than a nearby sixth form, and this was sometimes reflected in the way that new students spoke about their academic abilities (or their perceived lack of them). However, FE colleges can generally offer a much wider range of study options that can make them more appropriate for students who want to follow a particular pathway regardless of grades. Secondary teachers advising their students should be mindful of this; studying A-levels in a sixth form college with higher entry requirements may be viewed as more prestigious, but as we shall see in our case study, this might not be the right choice for all learners, regardless of ability. These hierarchies amongst institutions are also seen in the university sector, as discussed below.

Higher Education providers

Oxbridge and pre-1992 universities

Oxford and Cambridge constantly top university league tables and carry a formidably prestigious reputation. Both are steeped in tradition and have fiercely competitive admissions policies, requiring exceptional grades and successful performance at interview. Both are part of the Russell Group, a group of 24 UK universities describing themselves as 'world-class, research-intensive universities' (Russell Group, undated; unpaged). The Russell Group is a relatively new body, but the institutions that make up the group have long histories as universities; as well as Oxford and Cambridge, these include the University of Manchester (established in 1824), Queen's University Belfast (1845) and the University of Edinburgh (which can be dated as far back as 1583).

Despite the self-appointed nature of the group, it retains a cachet that makes it desirable to many students, including high numbers of international students – 32 per cent of Russell Group students are of non-UK nationality. Thus, students attending these prestigious universities may have additional transitional challenges in moving and adapting to a different country and culture as well as a different level of study. It is also easy to assume that students who have achieved the high entry requirements will adapt to the academic elements of transition more easily, although the range of assessments used in HE and the depth of knowledge needed means that this is not always the case.

Post-1992 universities and HE in FE

The term 'post-1992 university' is generally used to refer to institutions in the UK which obtained university status after the passing of the Further and Higher Education Act 1992. They are sometimes called 'new' universities, despite many of them having long histories as polytechnics or colleges, in order to differentiate from the universities discussed above. This explains why many cities have more than one university; Manchester, for example, is home to both The University of Manchester (a Russell Group member) and Manchester Metropolitan University (the former Manchester Polytechnic). A sense of hierarchy still remains, regardless of strong performances amongst post-1992 universities in university league tables, particularly when non-traditional measures are taken into account. A recent report from the Institute for Fiscal Studies in partnership with The Sutton Trust (IFS, 2021) ranking universities on their contributions to social mobility found that post-1992 institutions significantly outperformed more selective universities in accepting more students from low-income backgrounds who go on to become high earners.

These 'new' universities often carry lower entry tariffs than Russell Group universities, and attract a higher percentage of home students who live in the local area or who commute from neighbouring regions. The same is true of the growing number of FE and sixth form colleges offering degree courses, which are taught by college staff using college resources and facilities but ratified by an external university. As we have seen above with entry requirements for A-levels and BTECs, a less selective policy requiring lower entry grades can exacerbate prejudices around the perceived quality of a particular institution. Similarly, some 'new' universities remain associated with particular occupations as a result of their previous identity; York St John, for example, has its origins in a teacher training college founded in 1841 and remains associated with teaching and education (in public perception, at least), despite offering a wide range of courses.

It is important to challenge deficit narratives around choice of course and/or institution, whilst being mindful of specific transitional challenges. For example, it is easy to assume that learners living at home find the transition process easier in terms of managing social and financial changes – but home students often cite commuting costs and isolation from their peers as real issues. Additionally, 'new' universities attract more mature students (twenty-one or over at the start of their course, but often older), who may have family responsibilities not faced by their younger peers, and who are likely to have been out of the education system for a longer period of time. This can affect practical considerations such as childcare, as well as causing a lack of confidence that can make their transition to HE harder.

Key takeaways:

- Place matters!
- Not all courses and qualifications are available in all institutions.
- A sense of hierarchy remains amongst different types of institution that may affect a learner's experiences of the transition process.

Case study

The research reported on in this section took place in an FE college in England, anonymized as Northlands College of Further Education (NCFE). NCFE is one of 231 general further education colleges in England, and offers a wide range of courses at different levels.

As part of a qualitative case study, twenty-four students were interviewed individually, all aged between 16 and 19 and in their first year of a two-year course. Interviews took place between October and December, inviting participants to reflect on the transition from secondary school to college that each had recently undergone. Twelve of the participants were studying A-levels and twelve were studying a BTEC in either ICT, Childcare or Sport. Participants were asked three questions:

- why select their chosen course in preference to a different course or finding an apprenticeship,
- what their expectations of that course had been, and
- to what extent their experience had matched their expectations (Gregory, 2023).

Shared experiences of transition

A common theme was that the transition from secondary school to college had brought a sense of greater maturity and increased confidence. This took many forms: some participants spoke of academic maturity ('I've matured as a person as I've adopted a more organized approach to private study') and linked this with personal and social growth, speaking of feeling more confident in managing money, travelling independently, and being answerable to teachers for missed work and non-attendance rather than staff ringing their parents.

Positive social aspects of transition included finding a new friendship group at college. For most 16-year-olds, this transition marks their first opportunity to break with the friendship groups to which they have belonged for five years. Whilst this can be a terrifying thought, the participants spoke very positively of the chance to make new friends and forge a new, more authentic identity, reflecting who they had become rather than how others had perceived them from the age of eleven.

Finally, participants were almost universally interested in applying to university after college, suggesting that transition to college, as well as conferring social and personal benefits, is a valuable stepping stone on the road to higher education regardless of academic pathway. All twelve A-level participants spoke of going to university as a motivating factor in their choice of course, and ten of the twelve BTEC students were seriously considering applying. BTEC participants also showed clear awareness of the future workplace, with comments such as '[a BTEC in ICT] opens the door wider for going into an organization with more skills'. This positions vocational qualifications as delivering the skills and knowledge required to acquire a desirable job but also allowing the possibility of going on to further study – one participant said, for example, he had developed 'good skills' that would be useful both 'at uni and at work'.

Pathway-specific experiences of transition

Elsewhere, the data suggested students' experiences of transition to college had been affected by the academic pathway they had chosen, and the way it was perceived by influential figures in their lives – largely parents and teachers. Seven participants had been explicitly told by their parents or teachers that A-levels were a more desirable choice for students with particular academic ability or ambitions (in other words, because they were 'clever', as several participants commented). This made students anxious about their ability to cope with the requirements of such a seemingly academic qualification. Two of the participants noted the opposite problem – their teachers' assessment of their academic ability had led them to assume that A-levels would be easy ('a breeze'), and they were already struggling academically with the level of work required.

BTEC participants, meanwhile, began their accounts of transition in deficit mode, often reporting that they had been directed towards vocational qualifications by teachers as they had been less successful in exams than some of their peers: 'I was never very good at doing tests.' However, alongside these negative perceptions of their abilities emerged a more positive account of how choosing this particular pathway had allowed them to thrive by removing the pressure of exams and assessing their ability in a different way. Three of the BTEC participants had started an A-level programme but then switched to a BTEC a few weeks into the course. Far from being a second chance, the change of course was seen by these learners as a valuable move in terms of the 'constant, hands-on, practical style of learning' rather than the 'more theoretical A-Level, where they just teach you to pass an exam … you just regurgitate at the end of the year'. In other words, A-levels are not necessarily the right choice even for those who hold the required entry grades.

Implications for teaching and leadership staff

Secondary school teachers

As we have seen in our case study, learners preparing to transition into post-16 education are highly influenced by the advice of their teachers. There is statutory careers guidance available for schools (DfE, 2023), and the following points are also worth bearing in mind:

- Some knowledge of *all* the academic pathways available to students is desirable, as well as where students can go for further guidance.

- There is a need for objectivity in outlining the different qualifications available, particularly in terms of not presenting one route as a 'deficit' option, only suited to learners who have not excelled in exams.
- Whilst recognizing that teachers are under huge pressure to cover exam content, it can be helpful to begin encouraging students to develop the study skills needed for post-16 education.

Secondary school leaders

- Make time for staff development, so that teachers fully understand the qualifications available post-16.
- Consider how these different study options can best be communicated with parents and carers; for example, through guidance evenings with clear signposting to the full range of study options.
- Build links with local 16–19 providers. Sixth forms and FE colleges all offer information evenings or taster events for prospective students, and students should be encouraged to attend as many as they need in order to make an informed decision.

Teachers in 16–19 education

Staff in FE or sixth form colleges often know their students for less than two years. In that time, they need to help students transition from school to college, from GCSEs to level 3 study, and then prepare them for transition to the workplace or to further study.

- Bear in mind students may not have studied your subject before; students may think they know what is involved in A-level Psychology, for example, but in reality it may be nothing like they imagined.
- Remember to scaffold the skills needed for level 3 study. This may involve modelling an essay structure, showing students how to access library resources or making a checklist of what to take with them on work placement. Just because a learner has high GCSE grades does not mean they are ready for studying at a higher level.
- Students may ask for help writing their UCAS statements for university. This has traditionally been an area in which students from higher socio-economic backgrounds have been advantaged through the extra help they have received, so your input here can make a real difference to a student's progression.

Leaders in 16–19 education

- Most institutions allow learners to make changes to subjects/courses in the first few weeks; students should be made aware of this, and be given appropriate advice about the subject or course they wish to switch to.
- Information evenings and subject taster days throughout Years 10 and 11 can be very useful, as students' aims and preferences develop and change throughout their GCSEs.
- Build links with local HE institutions, to ensure students access relevant expertise about a range of study options.

Teaching staff in HE

While HE is often the end destination for post-16 learners, it is nevertheless vital for university teaching staff to understand the transition process their new undergraduates have undergone. The fact that learners can drop out of university without legal consequence arguably makes it even more important to support them as they reach the end point of their studies.

- Avoid making assumptions about prior knowledge or skills, particularly around notions of independent study.
- Remember that for many, social and physical transitions to HE represent an additional challenge on top of new academic expectations.
- Be sensitive to financial constraints. The transition to HE is an enormous financial commitment for many students, and care should be taken to signpost learners to relevant sources of help and advice.

University leaders

- Make sure teaching staff are aware where to refer students for pastoral, financial and academic support, and know the process for doing so.
- A range of activities throughout the year – applicant days, offer holder days, taster sessions – can help familiarize new students with the campus and its facilities before their course starts.
- Widening participation activities and summer schools are helpful for allowing learners to imagine themselves as university students.

Further reading

A number of books deal specifically with transition to higher education, including the following titles – although very few general titles consider the transition to sixth form or college.

Jones, H., Orpin, H., Mansi, G., Molesworth, C., & Monsey, H. (2023) *Transition into Higher Education*. St. Albans: Critical Publishing.

Matheson, R., Tangney, S., & Sutcliffe, M. (eds.) (2018) *Transition in, through and out of Higher Education*. Abingdon: Routledge.

References

CBI/Pearson (2015) Inspiring Growth: Education and Skills Survey 2015. London: CBI/Pearson. Available from: CBI-Pearson-Skills-survey-FINAL.pdf.

Department for Business, Innovation and Skills (2010) Fees and co-funding in further education in England: Banks review. Available from: https://www.gov.uk/government/publications/independent-review-of-fees-and-co-funding-in-further-education-in-england-co-investment-in-the-skills-of-the-future.

Department for Education (DfE) (2014) *GCSE and a Level Reform*. London: Department for Education. Available from: https://www.gov.uk/government/speeches/gcse-and-a-level-reform.

Department for Education (2023) Careers guidance and access for education and training providers. Available from: https://www.gov.uk/government/publications/careers-guidance-provision-for-young-people-in-schools.

Directgov (undated) AS and A Levels. Now archived. Available from: http://webarchive.nationalarchives.gov.uk/20100202100434/http:/direct.gov.uk/en/EducationAndLearning/QualificationsExplained/DG_10039018.

EducationUK.org (undated) The UK education system. Available from: https://study-uk.britishcouncil.org/options/education-system.

FE News (2022) 37% of all students now choosing to live at home. Available from: https://www.fenews.co.uk/education/37-of-all-students-now-choosing-to-live-at-home/

Gov.uk (undated a) School leaving age. Available from: https://www.gov.uk/know-when-you-can-leave-school.

Gov.uk (undated b) Further education courses and funding. Available from: https://www.gov.uk/further-education-courses/overview.

Gregory, E. (2023) Older and wiser than the schoolkids on the bus: The impact of academic transition on learner identity in an FE setting. *International Journal of Educational and Life Transitions*, 2(1), 1–13.

HESA (2023) Where do HE students come from? Available from: https://www.hesa.ac.uk/data-and-analysis/students/where-from.

Institute for Fiscal Studies (IFS) (2021) Universities are powerful vehicles for social mobility, with less selective institutions contributing more. Available from: https://www.fenews.co.uk/fe-voices/ifs-press-release-english-universities-ranked-on-their-contributions-to-social-mobility-and-the-least-selective-post-1992-universities-come-out-on-top/.

Ofqual (2014) An update on the reforms being made to AS qualifications and A-Levels. Available from: https://www.gov.uk/government/uploads/system/uploads/attachment_data/file/377915/2014-04-08-an-update-on-the-reforms-being-made-to-as-qualifications-and-a-levels__2_.pdf.

Pearson (undated) What is a BTEC? Available from: https://www.pearson.com/asia/learner/Qualifications/BTEC.html#:~:text=What%20is%20BTEC%3F,online%20and%20in%20the%20classroom.

Russell Group (undated) Our Universities. Available from: https://russellgroup.ac.uk/about/our-universities/.

UCAS (2022) UCAS undergraduate end of cycle data resources 2022. Available from: https://www.ucas.com/data-and-analysis/undergraduate-statistics-and-reports/ucas-undergraduate-end-cycle-data-resources-2022.

Universities UK (2023) International student recruitment data. Available from: https://www.universitiesuk.ac.uk/universities-uk-international/explore-uuki/international-student-recruitment/international-student-recruitment-data.

5

International Perspectives

Divya Jindal-Snape

Overview of chapter

This chapter focuses on primary–secondary school transitions of young people (YP), including those with additional support needs, and their transitions experiences. The chapter draws on, and presents, international perspectives and research, and sets the context for the importance of getting transitions policy and practice right for *all* YP. After discussing the policy and legislative context, I focus on the academic and social changes experienced by YP, and their impact on YP's transitions experiences. I discuss the factors that have been found to facilitate and/or hinder successful primary–secondary school transitions, including the role of different educational systems internationally. These are followed by a case study of a longitudinal study which provides further insights into some trends that have not been discussed before and/or are different from previous research. Relationships of YP with significant others (e.g. peers, teachers) are very important and have been discussed in detail. Finally, I have provided recommendations for primary and secondary schools' transitions practice and policy.

Current policy, legislation and context

Every year millions of YP start secondary school across the world, with UK government data showing that almost a million YP started secondary school in 2022–3 in the UK (Department for Education, 2023). Therefore, the importance of getting primary–secondary school transitions right cannot be overstated. This is especially important as previous literature suggests that primary–secondary transitions are problematic, with a negative impact on academic outcomes and decline in positive attitudes towards some subjects and increase in dropout rates (see Jindal-Snape et al., 2020 for details). Primary–secondary transitions have also been found to have a negative impact on YP's wellbeing due to stress and anxiety (Bagnall & Jindal-Snape, 2023). This is concerning as West and colleagues (2010) found that this can lead to long-term mental health issues.

However, as the majority of previous research has not mentioned the proportion of YP who actually experience difficulties, it is difficult to ascertain the actual gravity of the situation. It is important to highlight here that even one YP having a negative experience is cause for concern; however, the point I am making here is that it is possible that the unchallenged narrative of primary–secondary transitions being problematic, might act as a self-fulfilling prophecy.

For instance, in Australia, Waters and colleagues (2014) found that of the 2078 YP in their sample, 70 per cent reported that transition was easy/very easy. Similarly, in Scotland, Jindal-Snape and colleagues (2023) found that of their sample of 2559, 78 per cent YP had positive or moderately positive transitions (see Case Study section). In another Scottish small-scale study, data were collected when YP were in the final year of primary school (called P7), twice in the first year of secondary school (S1) and once towards the end of S2 (Jindal-Snape & Cantali, 2019). This study found that aspects of transitions that YP were looking forward to continued to stay positive in the secondary school (e.g. making friends, studying different subjects, better opportunities). However, the high level of concerns they had fell substantially once they started secondary school (e.g. about bullying, getting lost, not being able to make friends). It is important to note that their transitions were not linear; a few who had noted successful transitions in S1, highlighted that they faced problems when starting S2 without any support to facilitate their transitions.

However, irrespective of the country, research suggests that YP with additional support needs, are more likely to experience issues with their transitions (see Jindal-Snape et al., 2020 for more details). A large-scale study which analysed the Growing Up in Scotland (GUS) longitudinal dataset with a mixed sample found that YP with additional support needs were less likely to have a positive transition and more likely to have a negative transition than their peers who did not have any disclosed additional support needs. Of those who had additional support needs at either of two time points (penultimate year of primary school and first year of secondary school), 26 per cent experienced a positive and 32 per cent a negative transition. On the other hand, of their peers, 39 per cent had a positive and 19 per cent a negative transition. This provides some evidence to substantiate the claims of the studies with small samples.

Some studies reported that this was due to increased noise and hustle in larger secondary schools as well as acoustics and having to travel to secondary school, especially if distant. On the other hand, it is important to note that in one study, YP who had autism reported that they preferred the structured approach and routine of secondary school (see Jindal-Snape et al., 2020). Interestingly, in the context of Covid-19 bubbles, Saville and colleagues (2024) found that smaller group structure was effective in supporting YP navigate their transitions.

Legislation related to transitions of YP who have additional support needs

Most nations have legislation to make support for those with additional support needs (broader than SEND elsewhere) mandatory. In Scotland, The Education (Additional Support for Learning) (Scotland) Act (2004) (amended 2009) provides the legal framework for the provision of additional support for learning. It focuses on support being required for any reason, whether short or long term, determined by the specific learning needs of that young person. These can include, amongst others, factors related to disability or health, the learning environment, family circumstances, social and emotional factors, and English as an Additional Language (see Figure 5.1). It places key responsibility with the local authorities to support YP and provides clear guidance on transitions support with planning to start at least six months prior to a child starting primary school and secondary school. This is extended to at least a year for those making post-school transitions.

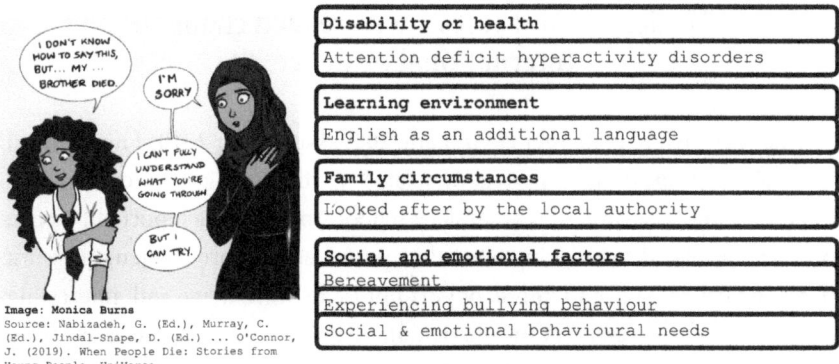

Figure 5.1 Examples of Additional Support Needs (The Education [Additional Support for Learning] [Scotland] Act [2004] [amended 2009]).

Similarly, in the United States, Individuals with Disabilities Education Act (IDEA, 2004) mandates that for any YP who has an Individualized Education Program (Individualised Education Programme) and is in K-12 education, transition planning should start at least a year prior to the young person turning sixteen. It places the duty on school to ensure that this planning is individualised and based on the YP's strengths, interests and preferences, and to notify the YP and parents of any upcoming meetings and involve them in any decision-making. You can find out more about supporting transitions for pupils with SEND in Chapter 6 of this volume.

Key takeaways:

- Majority of YP are likely to experience positive primary–secondary school transitions, most of the time.
- There is some evidence to suggest a negative impact on educational and wellbeing outcomes.
- YP who have additional support needs are more likely to have a negative transition experience and might require timely, targeted and ongoing support to navigate their transitions.
- Providing individualized transitions support to YP with additional support needs is a legislative responsibility of the education authorities and schools. Beyond the legislative duty, school leaders and teachers have responsibility to provide tailored, timely and shared transitions support to all YP as transitions can trigger additional support needs for some YP.

Academic- and assessment-related changes: International evidence

Previous research (e.g. Benner & Graham, 2009; West et al., 2010) found mixed views about transitions experiences related to the changes in curriculum, homework and assessment in secondary school. Some pupils reported positive experiences related to enjoying what they perceived as more challenging work in secondary school, and more opportunities to learn new and interesting things due to the diversity of the curriculum. However, some studies reported a 'honeymoon' effect with these views changing over time (see Jindal-Snape et al., 2020 for more details).

Where negative views were noted, they were related to:

- the lack of curricular continuity and progression
- decline in positive attitude towards some subjects
- reduction in academic engagement and academic motivation
- higher rates of absences
- increased academic difficulty
- high volume of homework
- academic skills related support needs rising
- concerns about assessment methods that were different from what they had experienced in primary school

The latter were also due to the decline in grades after starting secondary school. However, it is important to be mindful that when studies from different countries reported a decline in grades, neither the curriculum nor the assessment practices were the same even within one country or schools in the same region. For example, some studies used classroom assignments, some report cards and some state-wide administrative examinations to report on decline in educational outcomes. Therefore, it makes it challenging to treat these studies as giving us comparable results that can be relied upon.

Further, although a decline in grades, attendance and engagement was evident in some studies, we should be cautious as we do not know if this was actually due to the move to the secondary school and practices there. This becomes particularly evident when, as will be seen later, there are several other factors that can have an impact on transitions experiences, such as family background and school characteristics.

Key takeaways:

- There is some evidence of positive and negative impact of primary–secondary transitions on educational outcomes.
- It is important that there is curricular continuity but also some discontinuity between primary and secondary schools. However, instead of this being accidental, it has to be carefully planned by teachers in these schools.
- In the latter years of primary school and early years of secondary school, it would be useful to have at least some similarities in the assessment practices, with changes being gradual and over time.

Managing social and relational changes: International evidence

During primary–secondary transitions, relationships with several people might be in a state of flux, with the only constant being the family. Family is considered to be their most important support network by YP. However, we also know that families can sometimes raise YP's anxieties based on their own primary–secondary transitions experiences and 'fear' of entering a space where they might have had a negative experience (Jindal-Snape & Foggie, 2008). Further, due to their developmental stage, YP start looking for independence and the relationship dynamics might change leading to transitions for families too.

Similarly, relationships with teachers in primary and secondary schools can have the most impact on their transitions experiences. For instance, Jindal-Snape and colleagues (2023) found that a perception of the lack of fairness from teachers could have a detrimental impact on YP's transitions experiences. Other studies have also found that the relationship with teachers can be predictive of YP's wellbeing.

As can be seen, transitions, especially social and relationship transitions are important as well as very complex. Perhaps Jindal-Snape's (2016) proposed multiple and multi-dimensional transitions (MMT) theory might provide a way to understand these relationships and in which context they are changing the most. According to MMT theory, when YP move to secondary school, they are likely to experience multiple transitions (due to, for instance, change in relationships, change in pedagogical approaches of primary or secondary school teachers). However, these are happening at the same time in multiple contexts, e.g. school and home. Therefore, a focus on transitions experienced in school is not enough. These transitions are ongoing and can be exciting and worrying at the same time, as well as triggering transitions for significant others (e.g. their families, professionals). The significant others' own unrelated personal and/or professional transitions can also trigger YP's transitions. Therefore, we have to be mindful of not only the YP's transitions, but also that of their significant others, of which, a schoolteacher is one such significant other. If transitions of significant others are not supported, they might not be in a position to support YP with their transitions. Further, this can then have a profound impact on the YP's and others' social and relationship transitions.

It is important to highlight though that our recent research (Jindal-Snape et al., 2023) has found that most of the YP were positive about friendships going forward and reported making new friends. However, it is important to consider the context of the educational system their transitions were embedded in. In this case, in Scotland, normally most YP from a primary school go to a cluster secondary school; thereby retaining friendship groups, with 83 per cent YPs in the study reporting that they were attending secondary school with most or all of their friends. Although there is no conclusive evidence whether this has an impact on their educational and/or wellbeing outcomes, it might help reduce their (and their parents') anxiety before and once they moved to secondary school. In other educational contexts where YP do not go to the same secondary school as most of their primary school peers, concerns about losing old and making new friends have been raised, irrespective of the country (Jindal-Snape et al., 2020).

Key takeaways:

- Relationships can become a protective or risk factor for YP and their wellbeing.
- Relationships are in a state of flux during primary–secondary school transitions, and YP can be anxious about forming good relationships with peers and teachers in secondary school.

Impact of place, systems and environment: International evidence

In this section, we will consider five key aspects that can have an impact on transitions experiences of ***all*** YP.

Age at transfer to secondary school

The school starting age is different around the world; the age at which primary–secondary transitions take place can also vary. The age at the time of primary–secondary transitions is considered important as in most countries it coincides with puberty. In Germany, where transition to secondary school takes place after fourth grade (age 9 to 10 years), i.e., before the onset of puberty, Arens and colleagues (2013) conducted a study aimed to determine whether the declines in academic self-concept and self-esteem were related to the impact of transition or puberty and transition. Based on comparison of Grades 4 and 5 outcomes, they reported that those who moved to secondary school had lower levels of self-esteem and concluded that age at transition did not lead to the decline. However, the main problem with this study is that it investigated outcomes for two different cohorts rather than the same group of YP at two different time points.

Structural organization of schools

With the previous section in mind, it is important to consider the outcomes of organization of schools so that either YP move school at a different age (middle schools, in the United States and some parts of England), not physically moving schools (through-schools) and schools requiring a physical move.

In Australia, a study was undertaken by Vaz and colleagues (2014) to compare the academic competence scores of YP who went to three different types of schools, namely traditional primary–secondary schools, through-school *with* a middle school or a through-school *without* a middle school. They found that those YP who were in a through-school *without* a middle school had the highest post-school academic competence scores.

These findings resonate, to some extent, with a study conducted by Felmlee and colleagues (2018) in the United States with YP who physically moved to a secondary school; these YP had significantly lower levels of social integration and lower grades compared to those who had stayed at the same school. Similarly, in Israel, Madjar and colleagues (2018) found that YP who moved schools were more aware of the importance of socialization as compared to those who were in a through-school. This seemed to manifest, for those moving school, in a desire to demonstrate their ability to others (performance goals) over the desire for deeper learning (mastery goals).

However, another study reported different results. In a comparative study, Nielsen and colleagues (2017) studied the impact of the traditional system in Australia where YP moved to secondary school between the age of 12–13 and the through-school in Denmark where YP did not change schools at any point during schooling. They found that moving to a bigger secondary school in the Australian context was ideal for YP's age and stage related need for independence as well as an opportunity to create effective friendships due to a large group of peers to choose from. In contrast, they hypothesized that, in Denmark as YP stayed with the same peers, they might have been stuck with some they did not want to be friends with.

The findings related to middle school structure are inconclusive (middle schools are also known as junior high schools in some countries). Farmer and colleagues (2011), in their study of rural middle schools in the United States, reported that YP experienced less bullying as well as better social relationships. However, in contrast, Weiss and Baker-Smith (2010), also from the United States, reported that attendance at middle school resulted in worse academic outcomes as compared to other organizational systems.

Size of school

Researchers have investigated the impact of the size of primary and secondary schools on YP's educational and wellbeing outcomes in Australia and the United States. Vaz and colleagues (2014) found that YP in middle-sized schools (which they indicated as those with a roll of 375-95) had better outcomes than those in larger primary and secondary schools. In the United States, Benner and Graham (2009) found that an increase in secondary school size compared to primary school led to absences and decline in academic outcomes. They found that YP had a better sense of belonging in smaller, ethnically diverse schools. On the other hand, Nielsen and colleagues found that moving to a bigger secondary school was helpful for acquiring a larger friendship pool, school connectedness and socio-emotional outcomes in Australia.

The studies also emphasized that the size of the school in itself is not the only determining factor as, especially in the United States, it was noted that ethnically diverse schools with experienced teachers could also have an impact on transitions experiences.

Feeder schools and clusters

Similar to other factors, the impact of feeder/cluster schools is also inconclusive with a mix of outcomes noted. For instance, Langenkamp (2009) undertook secondary analysis of a large dataset in the United States, in which they compared systems where YP moved from a single primary to a single secondary school with where YP moved to a secondary school with multiple primary schools. They found that those who had transferred to a secondary school with multiple feeder primary schools were less likely to fail in the first year of secondary school. However, in other studies (Felmlee et al., 2018; Temkin et al., 2018), also in the United States, it was noted that moving to a secondary with multiple feeder schools was detrimental both academically and socially.

School climate and other systemic factors

Booth and Sheehan (2008) compared the impact of the school climate on primary–secondary transitions in the United Kingdom and the United States. They found that the YP in the United Kingdom reported feeling safer in their school than those in the United States. They also highlighted the impact of relationships with teachers and peers on the school climate, and the positive impact of involving YP in the transition process.

Other studies focused on the nature of the relationship between schools and local authorities with differences related to size and devolved responsibilities. For example, in the UK, Evangelou and colleagues (2008) found a difference in both the frequency and timing of the start of the interaction between primary and secondary schools was noted across different local authorities as well as the number of transitions-focused events (although the latter was also influenced by the resources available to schools). Also, the decision-making with regard to the secondary school a young person is likely to attend is also based on systemic factors, e.g., in Scotland a child knows what his local primary and secondary is and that they will move to those. However, there can be some uncertainty at times for YP with additional support needs; this has been found to raise the YP and family's anxiety levels with fewer opportunities to join the destination schools' transition activities and events.

Key takeaways:

- It was difficult to establish the impact of age at transfer.
- Findings about the benefits of school organizational structures were inconclusive.
- Findings regarding the size of school reported both positive and negative outcomes.
- The findings regarding the impact of one primary school or multiple primary schools feeding into a secondary school on the transition experience were contradictory.
- A supportive and safe school environment where YP were involved in the transition process was found to be important.

Impact of other factors on transition experiences: Case study

In Scotland, a large-scale study was undertaken by analysing a secondary dataset created as part of the GUS study (Jindal-Snape et al., 2023). Data analysed for the study were gathered from both children and parents, when the child was in the penultimate year of primary school (P6) and first year of secondary school (S1). The study included longitudinal data from 2,559 children who had responded at both school stages and had complete data. The findings were interesting, and a tentative trend can be seen (Figure 5.2). As can be seen, at the top is the percentage of YPs who had Positive, Moderately positive and Negative transitions. Below them are the trends that were found. For instance, girls can be seen on the left-hand side under Positive/Moderately Positive as they were more likely to have a positive transition than boys. Similarly, YP from a family where the parents were a couple were more likely to have a Positive/Moderately Positive Transition than those coming from a single-parent family. This suggests that gender, religious background, family makeup, older siblings, area of deprivation and so on can all make a difference to the probability of a YP having a positive/moderate/negative transition. Understanding this is important so that teachers can determine which YP, and families might need more transitions support.

Figure 5.2 Impact of key factors on YP's transitions experiences.

Positive Transitions (36%)	Moderate Transitions (42%)	Negative Transitions (22%)
Girls	←——→	Boys
Protestant/non-Catholic	←——→	Non-religious
Couple family	←——→	Single-parent family
No older sibling	←——→	Older sibling
High household income	←——→	Low household income
Area of low deprivation	←——→	Area of high deprivation
Parental education: Qualifications	←——→	Parental education: No qualifications
No additional support needs	←——→	Additional support needs
Child: Positive anticipated experience	←——→	Child: Negative anticipated experience
Feeling no pressure of schoolwork	←——→	Feeling pressure of schoolwork

Positive Transitions (36%)	Moderate Transitions (42%)	Negative Transitions (22%)
Involvement in sports, youth groups etc.	⟵⟶	No involvement in sports, youth groups etc.
Good communication and engagement from school	⟵⟶	Poor communication and engagement from school
Good parent–child relationship	⟵⟶	Poor parent–child relationship
Ease with making friends	⟵⟶	Difficulty making friends
Quality of friendship: Good	⟵⟶	Quality of friendship: Poor
Size: Large primary–large secondary	⟵⟶	Size: Small primary–small secondary
Perception of teachers being fair, esp. primary school teacher	⟵⟶	Perception of teachers not being fair, esp. primary school teacher
	Rural/Urban: no trend	

* Please note that the arrows are for illustrative purposes and these factors did not have a similar impact on the same number of children.

> ### Key takeaways:
>
> - Demographics and particular household and/or community characteristics can lead to YP being *more likely* to experience a positive or negative primary to secondary transition.
> - Understanding these *trends* can provide an insight into which children might need most support with during transitions.

Implications for primary school leaders and teachers

- It is important that all staff members in a primary school have discussions about what transitions and successful transitions mean to them and collect the views of YP and parents about their perspectives on it. It will be useful to consider whether transitions are ongoing and if so, in what way can they provide support to YP on an ongoing basis.
- Opportunities should be created in classrooms, at least a couple of years before the move, to discuss primary–secondary school transitions and successful transitions in an ongoing manner. These opportunities can also

be used to explore the myths and views about primary–secondary school transitions, and perhaps to alter the discourse to reduce any anxieties YP or families might have.
- YP's relationships with their primary school teachers, especially when they feel teachers are treating them fairly, were found to be really important in facilitating successful transitions. Therefore, it is important that teachers demonstrate fair and consistent practices.
- Collaboration is key! Early collaboration between primary and secondary schools is crucial, especially when YP have additional support needs. This is also a legislative requirement in some countries. Similarly, early collaboration with families is important so that there is some consideration of mitigating some of the factors related to families that have an impact on YP's transitions.
- It is important to be mindful of your own transitions and consider what support you need. This includes provision of training to support others and yourself. As training for supporting transitions is not uniformly provided by universities, it is important that this training is provided in schools as part of lifelong learning.

Implications for secondary school leaders and teachers

Some of the implications for secondary schools are the same as for primary schools. Additional ones are as follows:

- Provide opportunities for YP to visit your school a few years prior to the move. This should be ongoing and can take the form of YP using the gym and lab facilities at the secondary school. This might be difficult in some educational systems where there is no system of feeder and cluster primary and secondary schools.
- Visit primary schools and invite primary school teachers to your classes so that there can be a better understanding of the pedagogical approaches used in different schools at different stages.
- Create opportunities for YP to work in small groups with a view to creating strong friendships.
- Consider opportunities for good relationship building with teachers and other school professionals, keeping in mind that YP have to work with multiple teachers and do not get much time to bond with them.

Further reading and support

Jindal-Snape, D. (2016) *A–Z of Transitions*. Basingstoke: Palgrave.
This book includes entries on various types of transitions, theories and strategies. This is important as professionals need to understand these in the context of different educational and life transitions the YP are experiencing and how primary–secondary transitions can be affected or trigger future transitions. Each entry provides clear implications for professionals.

Jindal-Snape, D., Hannah, E.F.S., Cantali, D., Barlow, W., & MacGillivray, S. (2020) Systematic literature review of primary-secondary transitions: International research. *Review of Education*, 8(2), 526–66. https://doi.org/10.1002/rev3.3197.
This literature review article provides details of previous international research on the impact of primary–secondary school transitions on YP's experiences, and their educational and wellbeing outcomes. Information has been summarized in easy-to-understand tables. It is available to download freely.

Bagnall, C., & Jindal-Snape, D. (forthcoming) *Supporting Wellbeing during Primary-Secondary School Transitions: Advice for Parents, Caregivers and Teachers* (Ask the expert book series). London: Routledge.
This book distils research to provide easy-to-understand guidance for families and professionals, focussing specifically on primary–secondary school transitions.

References

Arens, A.K., Yeung, A.S., Craven R.G., Watermann, R., & Hasselhorn, M. (2013) Does the timing of transition matter? Comparison of German students' self-perceptions before and after transition to secondary school. *International Journal of Educational Research*, 57, 1–11.

Bagnall, C., & Jindal-Snape, D. (2023) Child self-report measures of primary-secondary transition experiences and emotional wellbeing: An international systematic literature review. *International Journal of Educational and Life Transitions*, 2(1), 1–31. Article 4. https://doi.org/10.5334/ijelt.35.

Benner, A.D., & Graham, S. (2009) The transition to high school as a developmental process among multiethnic urban youth. *Child Development*, 80(2), 356–76. doi:10.1111/j.1467-8624.2009.01265.x.

Booth, M.Z., & Sheehan, H.C. (2008) Perceptions of people and place young adolescents' interpretation of their schools in the United States and the United Kingdom, *Journal of Adolescent Research*, 23(6), 722–44. https://doi.org/10.1117/0743558408322145.

Department for Education (2023) Education and training statistics for the UK. https://explore-education-statistics.service.gov.uk/find-statistics/education-and-training-statistics-for-the-uk.

Evangelou, M., Taggart, B., Sylva, K., Melhuish, E., Sammons, P., & SirajBlatchford, I. (2008) *Effective Pre-school, Primary and Secondary Education 3-14 Project (EPPSE 3-14): What Makes a Successful Transition from Primary to Secondary School?* London: Institute of Education, University of London/ Department for Children, Schools and Families.

Farmer, T.W., Hamm, J.V., Leung, M., Lambert, K., & Gravelle, M. (2011) Early adolescent peer ecologies in rural communities: Bullying in schools that do and do not have a transition during the middle grades. *Journal of Youth and Adolescence*, 40(9), 1106–17. doi:10.1007/s10964-011-9684-0.

Felmlee, D., McMillan, C., Inara Rodis, P., & Osgood, D. W. (2018) Falling behind: Lingering costs of the high school transition for youth friendships and grades. *Sociology of Education*, 91(2), 159–82.

Individuals with Disabilities Education Act, 20 U.S.C. § 1400 (2004).

Jindal-Snape, D., & Foggie, J. (2008) A holistic approach to primary-secondary-transitions. *Improving Schools*, 11(1), 5–18.

Jindal-Snape, D. (2016) *A-Z of Transitions*. Basingstoke: Palgrave Macmillan.

Jindal-Snape, D., & Cantali, D. (2019) A four-stage longitudinal study exploring pupils' experiences, preparation and support systems during primary-secondary school transitions. *British Educational Research Journal*, 45(6), 1255–78. https://doi.org/10.1002/berj.3561.

Jindal-Snape, D., Hannah, E.F.S., Cantali, D., Barlow, W., & MacGillivray, S. (2020) Systematic literature review of primary-secondary transitions: International research. *Review of Education*, 8(2), 526–66. https://doi.org/10.1002/rev3.3197.

Jindal-Snape, D., Bradshaw, P., Gilbert, A., Smith, N., & Knudsen, L. (2023) Primary–secondary school transition experiences and factors associated with differences in these experiences: Analysis of the longitudinal growing up in Scotland dataset. *Review of Education*, 11(3), Article e3444. https://doi.org/10.1002/rev3.3444.

Langenkamp, A.G. (2009) Following different pathways: Social integration, achievement, and the transition to high school. *American Journal of Education*, 116(1), 69–97. doi:10.1086/605101.

Madjar, N., Cohen, V., & Shoval, G. (2018) Longitudinal analysis of the trajectories of academic and social motivation across the transition from elementary to middle school. *Educational Psychology*, 38(2), 221–47. doi:10.1080/01443410.2017.1341623.

Nielsen, L., Shaw, T., Meilstrup, C., Koushede, V., Bendtsen, P., Rasmussen, M., & Cross, D. (2017) School transition and mental health among adolescents: A comparative study of school systems in Denmark and Australia. *International Journal of Educational Research*, 83, 65–74. doi:10.1016/j.ijer.2017.01.011.

Saville, K., Leaton Gray, S., Perryman, J., & Hargreaves, E. (2024) Creating year 7 bubbles to support primary to secondary school transition: A positive pandemic outcome? *Education 3–13*, 52(1), 48–60. https://doi.org/10.1080/03004279.2023.2186977.

Temkin, D.A., Gest, S.D., Osgood, D.W., Feinberg, M., & Moody, J. (2018) Social network implications of normative school transitions in non-urban school districts. *Youth and Society*, 50(4), 462–84. https://doi.org/10.1177/0044118X15607164.

Vaz, S., Parsons, R., Falkmer, T., Passmore, A.E., & Falkmer, M. (2014) The impact of personal background and school contextual factors on academic competence and mental health functioning across the primary-secondary school transition. *Plos One*, 9(3): e89874. doi:10.1371/journal.pone.0089874.

Waters, S., Lester, L., & Cross, D. (2014) Transition to secondary school: Expectation versus experience. *Australian Journal of Education*, 58(2), 153–66.

Weiss, C.C., & Baker-Smith, E. (2010) Eighth-grade school form and resilience in the transition to high school: A comparison of middle schools and K-8 schools. *Journal of Research on Adolescence*, 20(4), 825–39. doi:10.1111/j.1532-7795.2010.00664.x.

West, P., Sweeting, H., & Young, R. (2010) Transition matters: Pupils' experiences of the primary-secondary school transition in the West of Scotland and consequences for well-being and attainment. *Research Papers in Education*, 25(1), 21–50.

Part 2

Holistic Approaches

6

SEND and the Role of SENCOs

Lorraine Petersen

Overview of chapter

This chapter examines the extra considerations and support required at transitional points for children and young people with Special Educational Needs and Disabilities (SEND).

The Special Educational Needs Coordinator (SENCO) is a statutory role that every school must have. The SEND Code of Practice (Department for Education, 2015; 6.84 to 6.94) clearly sets out the role of the SENCO including the day-to-day responsibility for the operation of SEN policy and coordination of specific provision made to support individual pupils with SEN, including those who have Education and Health Care (EHC) plans. The role of the SENCO is therefore key to successful transition and will need to work collaboratively with other professionals to ensure a smooth transition for this vulnerable group of pupils. The chapter draws on my own knowledge and experience of working with many SENCOs from all phases across England and parent carers who have had very different experiences of transition for their child. The chapter will consider the different points of transition from a child's entry into reception through to a student moving into post 16-education, employment and training. The case studies that I have included in this chapter will give examples of a child entering full-time education and one moving from primary to secondary school.

Current policy in SEND in England

The Equality Act (Gov.UK, 2010) sets out that no person should be discriminated against, including those with disabilities. This means that all educational establishments have to make reasonable adjustments to support SEND pupils in their school. The SENCO must ensure that all staff understand the individual needs of the pupils they teach and that alongside the high-quality teaching they provide for every lesson, they are also providing adaptations and adjustments to support these needs.

Chapter 3 of the Children and Families Act (Gov.UK, 2014) sets out the statutory requirements to support children and young people with SEND from zero to twenty-five. There are considerable duties in early years' settings, schools, post-16 institutions, local authorities and health and social care to provide appropriate, individual support for all those children and young people with SEND. This includes the duties of all these bodies to ensure that the needs are met from birth to age twenty-five, which includes transition between educational establishments.

The Special Educational Needs and Alternative Provision (SENDAP) Improvement Plan (DfE, 2023a) clearly sets out the importance of transitions for children and young people with SEND. As part of the Change Programme (DfE, 2023b), the government committed to providing good practice guidance to support consistent, timely, high-quality transitions for children and young people with SEND and in alternative provision. This would ensure all educational settings would have to follow specified guidance on effective transitions for SEND children and young people.

Since the disruption to education during Covid-19, there has been an increased concern around attendance and behaviour. The number of pupils who are persistently absent (missed more than 10 per cent) from school is around 20 per cent of the school population (DfE, 2024a). This is slowly declining but remains a major concern, as it is often those children and young people with SEND (especially those with Emotional, Social and Mental Health Needs) who are more likely to be absent for significant lengths of time. The term Emotional Based School Avoidance (EBSA) has replaced School Refuser, raising the issue around the lack of support for those children and young people who are experiencing mental health needs.

This is also reflected in the exclusions and suspensions data (DfE, 2024b, unpaged; Pupil Characteristics section) which indicate:

> *The rate of suspensions among those pupils who have an education, health and care (EHC) plan is 21.60 which is lower than for those with SEN without an EHC plan (SEN support) at 24.42. This compares to 6.38 for pupils with no SEN. The rate of permanent exclusions among those pupils who have an EHC plan is 0.20, which, like suspensions, is lower than for those with SEN without an EHC plan (SEN support) at 0.37. This compares to 0.07 for pupils with no SEN.*

Those pupils who are on SEND Support are at most risk of being suspended and permanently excluded.

The lack of high-quality transition from primary to secondary school could be one reason for this. Due to the global pandemic, during the summer terms of 2020 and 2021, schools were unable to offer as many face-to-face transition experiences as they would have liked. SENCOs were less likely to meet to have conversations about individual pupils and records may not have been passed on as quickly as they should have been. This resulted in pupils, especially those on SEND Support, not having their individual needs met from the start of each academic year. This may have left them vulnerable, anxious and unable to manage, resulting in low attendance and challenging behaviours.

Key takeaways:

- Schools should understand their legal responsibilities outlined in The Equality Act 2010 and The Children and Families Act 2014.
- Schools are expected to provide high-quality teaching and learning that is adapted and adjusted to meet individual needs – this includes the support they give at transition points.
- Attendance and behaviour may be impacted by poor transition opportunities.

Academic change and curriculum requirements

All schools have to adopt a broad and balanced curriculum that meets the needs of their pupils. Sitting alongside the curriculum is a national programme of assessment from the Early Years Baseline to General Certificate of Secondary Education (GCSE) at the end of Key Stage 4. All schools are required to follow these, resulting in a system that is extremely academic and tightly timetabled with very little flexibility in what they are able to provide on a daily basis.

The latest SEND Statistical Information (DfE, 2024b) indicates that 54.4 per cent of pupils with an Education, Health and Care Plan (EHCP) are now educated in our mainstream schools, meaning that schools are becoming more inclusive. In 2020, this figure was 48 per cent, indicating a significant increase in pupils with an EHCP now being educated in mainstream schools. This is also a result of the majority of our specialist settings being full: mainstream schools have to admit pupils with more complex needs. At a time when schools are encountering significant financial constraints and having difficulty recruiting new staff, this is an ever-increasing concern. Experienced and well-trained staff are vital to ensure that these pupils have their individual needs met.

The academic accountability measures that currently exist (SATs and GCSEs) are also a major stumbling block for full inclusivity across the education system. Whilst there is an expectation that all pupils will be able to achieve national expected standards in their SATs at the end of KS2 or eight GCSEs at the end of KS4, the ability to be fully inclusive is compromised. Not all pupils will reach these expected levels but whilst these are the accountability measures placed on schools, there will always be some schools who will make a case for why they are not able to meet an individual's needs based on how that pupil might affect their school attainment statistics. Unfortunately, for a small but ever-increasing group of children and young people with complex needs, this system is failing them.

Schools are having to think outside the box and are beginning to develop internal appropriate provisions and/or an adapted curriculum for those pupils having difficulty accessing a mainstream classroom. This might be based on a nurture- or trauma-informed approach. It usually requires extra space and a more calming and relaxed environment. Many pupils with Social, Emotional and Mental Health (SEMH) will thrive and learn in this type of environment. However, if a pupil has been able to access this type of provision, it is very important that this information is passed on at the point of any transition. Detailed information should be available about the type of support the pupil has had, what has worked effectively and what the consequences are if this provision is not in place. This is especially important at primary to secondary transition. SENCOs from primary feeder schools need to be working with the SENCO from their feeder secondary schools to ensure that they are fully aware of the type of provision an individual pupil might require.

Key takeaways:

- Mainstream schools are becoming more inclusive.
- Schools are developing their own internal provisions for pupils whose needs cannot be met in mainstream classroom.
- National accountability measures are not supportive of an inclusive education system.
- All SENCOs need to ensure that at transition, the receiving school fully understands the type of education that a pupil has received.

Assessment

All schools collect lots of data about their pupils. This can be based on any number of things, including summative and formative assessment, observations, attendance, behaviour and information from external agencies. For a pupil with SEND, there will be a great deal more. They may have:

- Individual Pupil Profiles – a document that outlines an individual's strengths and challenges, their likes and dislikes and information about what might help support their individual need – this would be produced with the pupil and their parents and reviewed regularly.
- Individual Learning Plans (ILP) – a document that outlines a pupil's educational needs and goals. ILPs are also known as Individual Education Plans (IEPs) or Individual Learning Improvement Plans. They will be reviewed termly, when progress is recorded and new goals are set.
- Provision Map – a document that shows interventions, support and additional staffing offered to learners within an educational setting, which is over and above their curriculum entitlement.
- Graduated Response records – Information about how the Access, Plan, Do, Review – Graduated Response process has been implemented for an individual pupil – this would be reviewed alongside the ILP.
- Copies of letters and information from specialists as well as academic progress information.

For pupils with SEND, schools will probably have carried out individual screening tests and specific assessments to identify pupils who are experiencing challenges with specific aspects of learning. The data collected from these are also vital to ensure that the pupil gets the best start in their new school.

Finally, information that the school has on any access arrangements that have been given to a pupil and information about their 'normal way of working' will ensure that the receiving school understands what is required to support the pupil. For example, if a child has learned to touch type in the primary school and has access to a laptop for all their lessons, they will need this reasonable adjustment to continue in secondary school. If this does not happen and the pupil is expected to hand-write everything, this will be a massive challenge for that pupil and may cause significant anxiety or challenging behaviour which could result in the young person not attending school.

At a transition point where the pupil is moving to another school, all of this information needs to be passed to the receiving school. Under General

Data Protection Regulation (GDPR), a school should not continue to hold information on a pupil who is no longer on their roll. More commonly, this is done by electronic transfer, but where paper-based records still exist, these should be forwarded either by hand or through secure post. This should be done before the end of the summer term to ensure that all relevant information is available for all staff prior to the start of the new academic year. Whichever medium a school uses, there should still be communication between SENCOs to ensure that the information that is being sent is put into context.

> ## Key takeaways:
> - All the SEND information that has been gathered over time should be transferred to the new school at transition.
> - Information about access arrangements and 'normal way of working' should be a high priority when passing on transition information.
> - Schools are required to make reasonable adjustments for pupils who may require them.

Social and relational changes

Home to the earliest years

Following the Global Pandemic in 2020, there have been a number of social and relational changes that have become concerns within schools. Primary schools have seen a significant increase in the number of children entering school with very poor speech and language and limited vocabulary. They are also seeing children with poor social skills and greater attachment issues. The Royal College of Speech and Language Therapists (RCSLT) reported that Covid-19 had impacted their services significantly (RCSLT, 2022).

As Chapter 1 has already observed, there are a number of different transition points in an educational setting. The initial transition point for a very young child may be leaving their loving parent/s and a safe and secure home to enter a childcare setting. Currently, all working parents are entitled to at least fifteen hours of free childcare for nine-month-olds and thirty hours for 3- and 4-year-olds (Gov.UK, 2024). This means that our Private and Voluntary Sector Early Years Providers and Childminders will be the first settings that these children will encounter.

Many of these settings now have a trained Early Years SENCO to support those children who may have additional needs. Local Authority Early Years Teams are also very involved with children at this young age. In one local authority, where I have recently done some work, over seventy children entered reception in September 2023 with an EHCP. This obviously will have an impact on their future schooling.

The majority of children begin their educational journey in an early years setting, as explored in Chapter 1, so it is crucial that we get transition right – if we do not, it can have a lasting impact on a child and their development. Case Study 1 illustrates an effective transition process later in this chapter.

The most important thing that schools can do at this point is to build very strong relationships with parent carers; they know their child best, so gathering as much information about the child and family is crucial. Find out about birth history, early childhood illnesses, family circumstances, likes and dislikes, the outcomes of the child's two-year check and any concerns the parent carer may have about their child's development. If possible, pay a visit to the home so you can see the child in their own environment. If Early Years staff have concerns about a child who may have additional needs, the SENCO should be involved as early as possible.

By building these strong relationships with parent carers, we are establishing a strong bond between home and school which hopefully will continue throughout their educational life. Parent carers are much more knowledgeable now about different needs and can very easily seek further information through the internet and social media. This has led to a significant increase in parental requests for diagnosis and 'labels' for their children. By building the initial relationships with parent carers, school and home can work in a co-productive way to ensure the best support for each individual child.

Key takeaways:

- The majority of children are in an early years setting from the age of three.
- Early years settings identify additional needs from a much earlier age.
- Covid-19 has had an impact on early childhood development.
- Working with parent carers and building a relationship with them is key to effective transition at this early stage.

Social transitions through primary education

Due to the rigidity of our education system, a child arriving from early years into a Year 1 setting is met with a much more formal and prescriptive curriculum. They will be expected to remain in their seat and do most of their learning from listening and watching the teacher – quite different from the experimental, curiosity learning they have been used to. They will have had at least a year of continuous provision and play-inspired learning that was adapted and adjusted to meet their individual needs. To ensure that this transition is smooth and effective for all concerned, it may support individuals if they continue to have access to the sorts of physical resources they had in reception – sand, water and construction toys, for example – with opportunities to continue to learn through first-hand play-based experiences.

If the relationship with parent carers was well established before the child entered education, the child can be better supported in the journey through the school, especially at this crucial point of a much more formal educational experience. There may be a small number of children who the school feels are not ready to move into Year 1 – this can be a very emotive subject for both school and parent carers – if communication has been excellent throughout early years, this will not be such a problem.

As the child moves from year group to year group, it is important that the school builds in sufficient time for children (and parent carers) to get used to the change of teacher and the environment they are working in. This will be an investment that will certainly save problems later on, particularly for those children known to struggle most with change. It is important to remember that although pupils remain in the same building for their primary years, classrooms may be different, teachers and their expectations will be different and their peers may be different (larger schools may move pupils into different classes), so there is still a significant amount of change from one year to the next. In some local areas, children will transition mid-way through their primary years – infants to juniors and first to middle, dependent on their schooling structure.

As mentioned previously, it is vital for the children with SEND that the SENCOs from both the sending and receiving schools communicate, preferably face-to-face, to share all information about the pupil and their needs. It is also very important that these pupils and their parent carers have opportunities to visit the receiving school, meet their teacher and get to understand the environment to which they will be going. This will require more than the one visit that is usually offered. Where the pupil has an EHCP, the receiving SENCO should be invited to the final annual review that takes place in the sending school. This will give the new school time and opportunity to organize staffing and space and adjust the environment if required.

Social transitions into secondary education

The move from primary to secondary school is probably the most traumatic for most young people and their families, especially so for those with a SEND. There are many challenges for those pupils entering Year 7, from remembering to bring all their resources each day to moving between lessons, topping up their lunch credit and catching the bus home. It also has to be remembered that some pupils will be coming from a school where very few of their peers have joined them and so they will need to develop brand new friendship groups – this can be very difficult at this key time in their lives. Case Study 2 highlights the importance of good transition opportunities for pupils with SEND.

Secondary schools are organized very differently from primary schools. The pupils have been used to one teacher for a whole year, based in one classroom with the same cohort of peers. For many this is a safe and secure environment in which they can flourish and develop. The move to a situation where they have a number of teachers, multiple classrooms, noisy and busy lesson changes and a possible inconsistency in behaviour management can lead to a very dysregulated pupil who is not able to function effectively throughout the school day.

If these anxieties are minimized and the transition is well managed, there are just as many benefits: more trust between the young person, parents and school; reduced anxiety for all concerned; fewer attendance and behaviour issues; clearer lines of communication; quicker identification of any problems; and less staff time needed to resolve concerns.

All secondary schools have transition programmes, but to ensure they meet the needs of all pupils, it needs to be more than a day showing children where the toilets are, meeting new staff and offering some example lessons. Once parent carers are informed about which secondary school their child will be attending, the school can start to make arrangements for additional transition opportunities for those pupils that require them. Waiting for the summer term when the pupil is in Year 6 is too late.

Good working relationships developed over time between primaries and secondaries ensure that children are prepared well in advance. The more staff can work together throughout a child's primary years, the better, with this collaboration reaching its peak in the Year 6 summer term at primary, so it blends seamlessly into the Year 7 autumn term at secondary. Physical visits are the most effective for pupils with SEND; these are probably best taking place when the school is quiet and empty in the first instance. This will help the pupil get used to the size and layout of the school site.

Schools are also being very creative with the use of technology, offering virtual tours, online maps and plans, blog posts from different teachers and welcome messages from current pupils in the school. This has the added incentive that pupils can watch in their own time, with family and friends and as many times as they need to. For example, in 2020, when pupils could not visit his school due to Covid-19, Steve Brice, a head teacher in Manchester, built his school in Minecraft over three weeks, in order to provide an engaging virtual tour for Year 6 students (CBBC, 2020).

It can be very helpful if the secondary school treats Year 7 as a 'transition year', taking all that is good from primary education and using it to ease the child into the secondary way of working without losing impetus or direction. It can also be very beneficial if primary teachers keep in touch with their previous Year 6 cohort and offer support and guidance to their secondary colleagues.

One of the challenges that often occur at this time is that schools concentrate on a smooth transition for all those pupils with an EHCP. Unfortunately, it is often the pupils on SEND Support that do not get the same amount of support at this crucial time. This may be why the data shared previously for exclusions and suspensions is so high for those on SEND Support – they did not get the transition support that they needed.

One of the major barriers that secondary schools face is building strong relationships with families. Parent carers are not often at the school gate and do not engage in daily communication in the same way they can at primary school. Many schools feel that by the time a pupil moves to secondary education, they need to have an arm's length approach to parent carers to ensure their child begins to gain independence for later life. This may be the case for the majority of pupils, but for those with SEND, having regular check-ins and home-school communication is vital to ensuring the pupil's individual needs are being met.

Parent carers with concerns can often feel disenfranchised and feel that they are not being heard. This can result in animosity and parents who feel they have to challenge and 'fight' for what their child might need. Engaging parent carers at the point of transition will hopefully support a positive relationship when the school and home are working collaboratively to ensure the pupil's needs are being met.

Social transitions into post-16 education, employment or training

Planning for post-16 transition has to start early. Offering opportunities, careers advice and support throughout the secondary school years will help all pupils to find their right path as they choose GCSE subjects and post-16 settings. For those with an EHCP, the Year 9 annual review will be key, particularly now that plans can support a young person up to the age of twenty-five. From Year 9 onwards, the local authority must make sure that the annual review meeting considers what provision is required to help a pupil (and their parent carers) to prepare for adulthood and independent living.

It is very important to keep lines of communication open with parent carers as they will also be concerned about the future for their child. There may also be conflict between what the parent carer wants and expects and what the pupil wants.

Key takeaways:

- Pupils moving from Early Years to Key Stage 1 may require a more play-based curriculum as part of their transitional arrangements.
- Although most pupils will transition at aged eleven, some pupils will transition at age seven, eight or nine (depending on the education structure in your local authority).
- Engagement with the pupil and parent carers as early as possible is essential.
- The transition process for pupils with SEND should be well planned between both settings.
- The Year 9 Annual Review is an important transition point for pupils with an EHCP.

Impact of place

All parent carers have the right to a mainstream education for their child with SEND (DfE, 2015). The majority of parent carers will want their child to be in a local school with their friends. It is really important that mainstream schools use their best endeavours to educate a pupil with SEND. Fully inclusive schools will find this very easy and will make adaptations and adjustments to ensure that a pupil's needs can be met.

For pupils with an EHCP, decisions about future placements would be discussed at annual review. It is imperative that any schools that may be being considered to take a pupil are invited to the final annual review prior to transition. That will give the receiving school the opportunity to find out more about the individual needs but also to be able to state whether they think they will be able to meet needs within the mainstream setting. If parent carers are seeking specialist provision, then an amendment to the EHCP would be submitted to the local authority and they would consult with the appropriate specialist provisions to see if they are able to take the pupil at the point of transition. In the current climate, many of the specialist provisions are full, and it may be that the mainstream schools are instructed to take the pupil. If this is the case, the SENCO would need to put a case together as to why they cannot meet the need or preferably what adjustments they would need to put in place and the cost of these.

It is the local authority's duty to ensure that the provision outlined in the EHCP is available and funded. If the decision is for the pupil to transition to a specialist setting, then it is still very important that additional support is given to ensure that this is as smooth as possible. It is highly likely that the pupil will be moving to specialist provision without any of their friends. The environment of a specialist provision will be very different, smaller classes, more adult support and pupils with a diverse range of additional needs.

For those pupils on SEND Support, transition can be much more challenging. If the sending and/or the receiving school is not supportive of the additional transition processes that have been mentioned throughout this chapter, it can mean a very difficult start for some pupils. This can often happen when a secondary school has a significant number of feeder schools and they have difficulty in visiting and meeting SENCOs from all of them. The use of technology for the transfer of files and virtual meetings might be an answer to this. Being able to have an hour's conversation between two SENCOs via a virtual platform would enable them to share all relevant information – some of which may not be written down.

Key takeaways:

- All parent carers have a right for their child to be educated in a mainstream school.
- For pupils with an EHCP, the decision about school placement will follow an annual review.

- It is the local authority's duty to ensure that the provision outlined in the EHCP is available and funded.
- Pupils on SEND Support will require additional support at transition to ensure they settle well into their new school.

Case studies and interviews

The following case studies are based on two pupils that I have known from schools that I have worked with. They set out how the schools worked with parent carers and external agencies to ensure a smooth transition for both pupils.

Case Study 1: Transition from home to early years setting

George is a three-year old boy who has had a physical disability from birth. He is able to walk with the aid of a walking frame. He has been at home with his parents (Mother at home full-time) since birth. His mother is going back to her job as a teaching assistant and so they are looking for full-time (thirty hours) provision at a local nursery. The nursery is very happy to admit George, but wants to ensure his safety and that of the other children.

The transition programme consists of:

A meeting with the parents to discuss George's needs.

A home visit to get to know George in a familiar setting.

George and his parents visit the setting when no other children are present.

The setting carries out a risk assessment on the environment and shares with parents.

The setting discusses George's needs with the Physiotherapist and Occupational Therapist that have been supporting him at home.

The setting ensures that it is fully accessible or reasonable adjustments are in place.

George visits the setting for a short period of time for a number of days to meet the other children and staff.

Staff adjust the provision as required to meet need.

George begins his full placement at the start of the new term.

Case Study 2: Transition from primary school to secondary school

Suzanne is a ten-year-old girl who has a diagnosis of Autistic Spectrum Condition (ASC) and attention deficit hyperactivity disorder (ADHD). She has been in mainstream school since reception and has coped really well with additional support. The primary school is very aware of her needs and makes adaptations and adjustments when required. Suzanne's parents are very concerned about her transition to secondary school – they had considered a specialist setting but their local secondary school has an autism base which they decided would be the better option as she would be able to stay with her friends. The SENCO from the secondary school was invited to Suzanne's annual review and was able to contribute to the discussion about her future educational journey. Following the annual review, the secondary school was named in Section I of the EHCP. A robust transition plan was developed between Suzanne, the parents and both schools.

The plan set out the following activities:

Suzanne and her parents to visit the secondary school one afternoon after the school had closed to walk around the building with both SENCOs. A virtual tour was available on the secondary school website and this was followed on the actual walk around. A plan of the school was given to Suzanne so that she could follow on her tour. Suzanne would then be able to refer to the virtual tour and plan whenever she felt anxious about the transition.

The Lead Teacher from the autism base to visit Suzanne at her primary school and spend some time getting to know her.

Suzanne and her parents to spend half a day in the autism base with other students around.

The two SENCOs to meet face-to-face to share information and discuss Suzanne's needs.

Once the secondary school knows who will be supporting Suzanne, a visit can be organized for them to meet.

Suzanne to take part in all the other transition arrangements with her peers.

Suzanne will be in a tutor group with at least one of her friends from primary school.

Suzanne is given her timetable and resources and equipment list during the summer term before transition.

Adjustments are put in place in regard to uniform due to Suzanne's sensory needs.

On the first day of term, Suzanne's support assistant meets and greets and they go to the autism base together – this will continue for as long as required.

The SENCO from the primary school checks-in early in the autumn term to see how Suzanne has settled.

Implications for teaching and leadership

- In pre-school settings, staff should ensure that they gather as much information as they can from parent carers prior to their child starting in a setting. This might include birth history, childhood illnesses, likes and dislikes and developmental milestones. This will allow the setting to begin to assess the needs of an individual child prior to entry.
- On moving from Early Years into KS1, teachers should consider the options for pupils that require a more play-based curriculum in Year 1. Many pupils with SEND may not be ready for the more formalized education expected in Year 1.
- All schools should continue to develop strong relationships with parent carers. This includes meeting with them regularly (at least three times per year) to discuss progress, goals and next steps.
- Each year, senior leaders and SENCOs should ensure that the receiving teacher has a complete understanding of the needs of individual pupils – especially if they have an EHCP.
- Transition for SEND pupils should begin as soon as parent carers are aware of which school their child is going to be attending. This will give both settings the ability to set up bespoke transition packages for those who require them. If transition information (virtual tour, photographs of key staff etc.) is available online, then giving parent carers links as soon as possible.
- Senior leaders may wish to consider Year 7 to be a transition year, especially for SEND pupils. This might include offering a more primary-based approach (one teacher for most subjects in one classroom) for the first part of the academic year.
- Senior Leaders and SENCOs must ensure that all staff have the relevant experience and training required to support pupil's individual needs. Regular SEND training should be an integral part of school continuing professional development.
- It is very important that the SENCO of the receiving school attends the final annual review in the current school for a pupil with an EHCP.

Further reading

Secondary school SENCO and EEF learning behaviour specialist Kirsten Mould explains how schools can tackle the challenge of supporting pupils through times of change and transition:
https://educationendowmentfoundation.org.uk/news/eef-blog-supporting-pupils-through-transitions-a-trio-of-challenges.

Morgan, F., & Costello, E. (2023) *Square Pegs: Inclusivity, Compassion and Fitting in – a Guide for Schools.* Carmarthen: Crown House Publishing. Over the last few years, changes in education have made it increasingly hard for those children who don't 'fit' the system – the square pegs in a rigid system of round holes – this book guides leaders and teaching staff through the most effective ways to address this challenge.

References

CBBC (2020) Minecraft: A head teacher used the game to create a virtual secondary school tour for kids joining Year 7. Available from: https://www.bbc.co.uk/newsround/53373921.

Department for Education (2011) Teachers' standards. Available from: https://assets.publishing.service.gov.uk/media/61b73d6c8fa8f50384489c9a/Teachers__Standards_Dec_2021.pdf.

Department for Education (2015) The SEND code of practice. Available from: https://www.gov.uk/government/publications/send-code-of-practice-0-to-25.

Department for Education (2020) Headteachers' standards. Available from: https://www.gov.uk/government/publications/national-standards-of-excellence-for-headteachers/headteachers-standards-2020.

Department for Education (2023a) SEND and alternative provision improvement plan. Available from: https://www.gov.uk/government/publications/send-and-alternative-provision-improvement-plan.

Department for Education (2023b) SEND and alternative provision improvement plan. Available from: https://www.gov.uk/government/publications/send-and-alternative-provision-improvement-plan.

Department for Education (2024a) Pupil attendance in schools – Week 29. Available from: https://explore-education-statistics.service.gov.uk/find-statistics/pupil-attendance-in-schools.

Department for Education (2024b) Suspensions and permanent exclusions in England. Available from: https://explore-education-statistics.service.gov.uk/find-statistics/suspensions-and-permanent-exclusions-in-england.

Gov. UK (2010) The Equality Act. Available from: https://www.legislation.gov.uk/ukpga/2010/15/contents.

Gov.UK (2014) Children and Families Act. Available from: https://www.legislation.gov.uk/ukpga/2014/6/contents.

Gov. UK (2024) Hundreds of thousands of parents can now access 15 hours free childcare for 9-month-olds – how to apply. Available from: https://educationhub.blog.gov.uk/2024/09/02/how-to-claim-15-hours-free-childcare-code/.

Royal College of Speech and Language Therapists (2022) The sustained impact of COVID-19 on speech and language therapy service in the UK. Available from: https://www.rcslt.org/wp-content/uploads/2022/01/Sustained-Impact-of-COVID-19-Report-RCSLT-January-2022.pdf.

7

Engaging Families and Communities in the Transition Process

Claire Wilkinson

Overview of chapter

This chapter examines the process of engaging families and communities in the transition process with a focus on the transition through secondary school to post-16. The focus of the chapter is broadly at the expectations of the education system while also comparing this to the perceptions of parents and how they see the importance of their impact and influence in the process. While exploring the processes that young people will experience, the chapter will consider inequalities, perceived or otherwise, between immigrant families and those who are UK born, and how the difference between these communities can affect the aspirations, engagement and effectiveness of the education system in enabling effective transitions for young people. Reay (2008) reviewed how education had changed and suggested that the attendance of parents at school events should not always be considered as engagement. She suggests that the system is constructed to reflect the middle-class family and the structure of achievement that fits a middle-class ideal. However, a working-class family may attend events and respond to requests from teachers and schools, but the education system does not recognize or respect the barriers for these families, and consequently, parents from working-class backgrounds can be at odds with the ideas of the school. If the experiences of working-class parents when they were children were negative, it may influence their perception of school expectations.

The chapter's case study considers parental engagement in rural communities with a rising immigrant population and the impact of this on the process of parental engagement to ensure a supportive and informed structure to the decision-making process for young people. The study is focused on a secondary school with an immigrant population of 40 per cent, in a rural town in the East Midlands, and examines how the challenges of a blended community with diverse lived experiences can provide either supportive transitions for their young people or can provide an oppositional narrative that disengages their young people from the transitional process. Therefore, the chapter looks to provide insight into overcoming barriers experienced by the young person and engaging parents in the process of transitions regardless of their educational background and argues that the educational system must strengthen their relationships with parents to allow for wider support from within the community by valuing parental importance as stakeholders in the transition process.

Current policy contexts in England

The Education Endowment Foundation (2024) defines parental engagement as 'teachers and schools involving parents in supporting their children's academic learning' and suggests that progress is made for children where a school effectively manages this approach. The Department for Education has cited research such as Carter (2017) as evidence that any policy on parental engagement, regardless of immigrant or UK-born status, is only effective when employed from the early years stage of education from the outset. The Department for Education (2017) states that mainstream secondary schools are most challenging of all the pre-16 sectors to gain parental engagement and suggests that non-judgemental approaches are part of how to change this relationship.

The link between poverty and disadvantage and engagement from children and parents is mentioned within the Department for Education's guidance for school leaders on using Pupil Premium (DfE, 2017), acknowledging that attainment gaps have grown during the pandemic and that all internal strategies should be underpinned by the engagement of parents and families to ensure all needs are met. The Education Endowment Foundation (2021) explored the challenge of parental engagement and found that the aims of government education departments across ten countries showed the same issues when reaching secondary age, in that parental engagement drops at this point and that transitions need to be tailored to the changing responsibilities of parents and carers once their children reach this stage of their education. The research suggests that where schools take a flexible approach to engaging parents, the benefit to pupils is around four months of progress.

This could be argued from a school perspective as a limiting factor of increasing strain on reducing budgets. Where a school is local-authority maintained, they are required to report their financial health each year to the local authority. The pressures on meeting increasing wages, maintaining building and adjustments to the curriculum are draining funds that could be redirected to the most vulnerable groups within our schools. This can limit opportunities offered to pupils who are disadvantaged and in turn can lead young people to look at options they perceive as safer when considering transitions from secondary education.

Key takeaways:

- Parental engagement drops during secondary education.
- Implementing policy needs to include parental engagement.
- Financial challenges within schools can create barriers for engagement.

Managing academic and curriculum changes

In a post-pandemic landscape, the return to GSCEs being measured as before but without the aspirations and role models of students who have experienced these transitions has impacted secondary progress throughout the transitional stages from key stage 3 to 4 and through to choices for next steps. The curriculum requirements and measurements for schools in the results tables do not reflect the requirements of some post-16 settings. Where young people are told there is no need to worry if they do not pass GCSEs and that colleges will find a route for them regardless, this provides a challenge to find an effective process between providers to work for the educational common goal. The impact on parental and pupil engagement can be affected by these unconditional offers and weaken the relationship with school in the run up to final exams when the motivation and engagement of the child and their parents offering support is influential on the child's success. Solutions offered in research include enhanced transition, community projects and events to draw together all stakeholders. Smyth (2020) theorizes that this is further influenced through parental educational experiences and that their influence on engagement with education is significant by the time their child is thirteen.

The increased use of online communications and use of platforms accessible by phone apps for parental engagement have been implemented during and post the Covid-19 pandemic and have impacted the relationships between the parent and the schools. In some cases, these have been positive, with engagement from parents in ensuring that their child accessed their education during the pandemic. However, upon returning to face-to-face schooling, there have been challenges for all stakeholders. Ariani and colleagues (2022) researched the cultural challenges in rural communities and found that progress and respect between all stakeholders in education including parents would benefit from understanding the values that are culturally important and building them into the curriculum development and delivery. By acknowledging all members of the community and ensuring they are reflected in the planning of academic events, showcasing the benefit of different forms of post-16 academic and career routes, the wider community will see the value in their engagement with education.

Rising cost of living and strain in local communities provide disadvantaged families with challenges at home to find effective ways of supporting their child in accessing learning expected outside of the classroom. The home learning methods that are commonplace in mainstream secondary schools require multiple hours of access to online materials or use of apps to support progress. Green (2020) found that one in five children from disadvantaged backgrounds did not have access to a home computer, putting the child already at risk of falling behind their peers and leaving parents feeling that their circumstances have not been considered. This study further evidences the strain in the relationship between parents and the education system's expectations, where parents are unable to meet the home learning requirement; the sanctions placed on their child will place strain on their own relationship. To allow for parents to willingly engage, the education system needs to seek out opportunities to redress the balance for those who are disadvantaged.

Key takeaways:

- Changes in curriculum are alienating the most disadvantaged families.
- The strain between cultures in the community impacts the engagement with education in disadvantaged areas.
- Children in disadvantaged areas struggle to access learning outside of the classroom.

Assessment

Parental buy-in is important to ensure that the child is taking the assessment and revision seriously to allow them to make informed choices for their options. The assessment process in secondary school is perceived to be higher stakes than the assessment in primary. In part, this is due to setting and links to future GCSE grades and the influence this can have on future academic journeys and job prospects. The grades that the child gets within key stage 3 will potentially limit the options available to them at key stage 4. For those with disadvantaged backgrounds or immigrant children who are still learning the language, this process can be demoralizing and lead to their disengagement and apathy from the outset of transition. Jerrim (2023) found that the high-stakes testing approach often resulted in grades that were not in line with a child's ability, and this would lead to frustration for children and increased anxiety.

The approach that schools take in explaining the importance of developing resilience in these tests is part of the communication needed to garner parental support in the process. With parental engagement and strong teacher-parent relationships, a narrative can be developed around the importance of commitment to achievement which can be relayed both at home and in school. This will build a child's confidence and look to engage them positively in assessments to enable reliable transition points and effective setting and support.

Rising numbers of suspensions and exclusions in mainstream schooling as reported by Explore Education Statistics (2024) show that in the academic year 2022–3, the increase in suspensions took the figures to 9.33 per 100 pupils and 0.11 per 100 pupils for permanent exclusions. The impact of this makes consistent and reliable assessment hard to complete and in turn does not support the building of resilience and confidence in the child. They are also a further strain on difficult relationships with parents dealing with the behaviour of their child. Making decisions around options and the transition into key stage 4 becomes difficult. Anderson (2020) surmised that where policy and practice was aimed at reducing suspensions and building confidence in accessing education, there was a significant increase in attendance for those individual pupils and their aspirations to achieve in assessment were raised. There is a need to develop social understanding for children and to provide the support to develop positive relationships that will enhance their planning with their parents and school to make their choices; this in turn will fuel their desire to achieve in the assessments needed to understand learning difficulties and gaps. When schools have a child-centred approach to planning assessments, positive relationships and engagement are more likely to be achieved.

> **Key takeaways:**
>
> - High-stakes testing in secondary can lead to anxiety.
> - Low-stakes testing and celebrating successes have impact on engagement.
> - Looking at child-centred approaches can increase engagement and resilience.

Managing societal and relational changes

The changes that exist for the child when entering secondary school can be daunting for them and their parent, with expectations of no longer walking a child to the gate, attending fewer events or assemblies and with the changing narrative of responsibilities placed on the role of the child and their readiness for the day at school. Bagnall and colleagues (2020) found that the transition from primary to secondary did not consider that the viewpoint of all stakeholders could have impact on attendance and engagement. The right approach from the outset, when communicating and providing days in the new setting to allow the child to assimilate to their new expected roles within a secondary, was considered key to helping build strong relationships from the outset with the parents.

For young people who now experience a world with enhanced use of technology, the ways schools can use this for positive communication with their parents through online systems, giving updates throughout the day, can reassure them to know that, despite possible phone use restrictions, their parent is still able to access their successes. Pollard and colleagues (2023) found that to establish and maintain positive relationships with parents in the secondary education sector, teachers need to establish consistent and clear communication that includes positive and negatives, alongside offers of support and guidance where parents are struggling with their child's engagement. Where teachers and school leaders use reflective approaches and respond positively to feedback, trust and strong relationships are built despite the change from a single point of contact to multiple teachers when moving from primary to secondary.

The changes for the child can be overwhelming when they have been at primary settings with small numbers and with one teacher for an academic year and then in contrast they are entering a much larger setting with multiple teachers, room changes and needing to form new peer relationships. Goetz and colleagues (2021) explored the impact of teachers on this transition and found that where the one teacher became a positive point of contact, either as a form tutor or a trusted member of staff, the children were able to use them as a mentor and a guide to how well they were integrating into their new setting.

Key takeaways:

- The change in the size of setting needs to be planned for using transition visits to build confidence.
- Communication with parents will ensure any worries are shared and resolved as soon as possible.
- Using a single point of contact for support will help bridge the gap between primary and secondary relationships for the child.

Impact of place

Limited options in the community

One of the key foci within the transitions both at the start of secondary and when making the move to further education is to engage the children and their parents in looking at opportunities within the area and to look at how choices such as options will help shape that journey. This part of the transition process is affected by the availability of courses within the local area; where this is limited, it can impact the engagement of the child in their education but also link to their parent and their own aspirations for their child. The challenge faced by secondary schools is also impacted by the changing of the offer for key stage 5, with the introduction of new courses such as T-Levels, that take time to establish themselves and to prove their worth. However, there is an additional challenge to help support parental understanding of these courses to enable their own conversations with their child when discussing their educational choices.

Where parents may still be struggling to adjust to the 9–1 grading approach of GCSEs, the introduction of new post-16 qualifications such as T-Levels may further alienate them from a system that they are not confident with. Therefore, they may feel they are not well informed and unable to help their child in making these key decisions such as options and next steps. Posey-Maddox and Haley-Lock (2020) explored the needs of families and how schools can improve their engagement and found that one size does not fit all; when a school considers the needs and situations of individual families, they can tailor the information and support to help them access the information they need to be active in transitions and choices with their child. However, the challenge with large secondary schools is that the numbers of parents can be overwhelming, and it is difficult to build that knowledge without considerable time passing. The use of pastoral managers and support staff can be useful in establishing initial contact to identify those families in need of extra support that have not been identified during the primary to secondary transitions.

Parents of low socio-economic status, who are employed and are confident of what they can offer their child in the world of work, may provide a narrative at home that does not lead to positive engagement from either the child or themselves. Furthermore, where the parent is unemployed and found it difficult to gain regular employment in the area, their lived experiences may lead to narratives that are not supportive or encouraging when discussing education and transitions to next steps. This needs to be challenged through educational events and communications, as outlined in the case study presented later in the chapter.

Inequality within education

The aspirations of children and the engagement of parents and the wider community are linked to the affluence and opportunity in the area. There are links between working-class and disadvantaged family narratives and fear of the debt that future educational choices will bring a child when they reach this stage of their academic journey. Hornby and Lafaele (2011) researched how schools could map the needs of parents and children to build a picture of emerging needs within the community and resources and support that they could access for individuals or groups to tackle inequalities. The earlier that this mapping is completed, the more time can be applied to researching proven methods to overcome any barriers. The impact of investment in breaking down these barriers and providing opportunities can be beneficial in demonstrating to families how success in secondary education can support accessing financial support for post-16 study and is one example of opportunities available to challenge the impact of disadvantage as a limiting factor.

Links with the community

Where the range of post-16 options and opportunities in the local area are limited, it can be difficult to maintain momentum and support from parents who may be disillusioned by their own experiences. To allow the impact to be minimized, it is important to gain the support and engagement of local colleges and post-16 facilities and of businesses able to offer apprenticeships to generate the interest of pupils and parents in engagement and success. This is part of a strategy suggested within the case study that is shown to be effective in sparking interest and deepens the relationship of parents with the school and their child's education from transition to primary and throughout secondary, especially where this is nurtured from the outset of open evenings and enrolment with the school. By engaging the community through showcase event and work experience and cultural capital opportunities, the children become immersed in the community and the parents see the time and dedication from the community, which in turn generates ambition and breaks down the barriers that impact engagement. Brown and Souto-Otero (2020) found that where work experience and future transition choices were linked to the local communities and their job markets, employers found job readiness more important than the qualifications. For schools to make use of this data and still encourage achievement, they must incorporate these skills into career planning as well as providing a challenging and ambitious education.

Key takeaways:

- Support with understanding the transition journey through the key stages will help parents and children prepare.
- Investing in breaking down barriers for disadvantaged students can impact on future success
- Engaging children with community in events and work experience will prepare them for future transitions.

Case study: Parental engagement in a rural setting

The study carried out was based in a rural community in Lincolnshire, at a mainstream secondary school, with the local community facing multiple challenges such as high unemployment, low pay and seasonal work, cultural challenges due to high immigration in the area and cultural clashes between UK-born and immigrant families. The study considers the challenges that come with increasingly diverse communities, challenging cultural resistance to education, disillusionment of parents that impact the transitions and aspirations of the young people within the community. The study, carried out as a PhD thesis, comprised thirty interviews in total, fifteen of which were with UK-born parents and fifteen with immigrant parents. These interviews were semi-structured and carried out by a trusted staff member whose role was to provide community support and to understand the barriers to parental engagement.

One of the challenges the parents expressed in the interviews was that they felt unable to engage in a system that they didn't feel represented their lifestyle as a parent, the wider community, or the best interests of their child. One parent expressed, 'my child is told to aim to be anything other than like me, it makes me feel like the school has no respect for jobs that don't need qualification with high grades'. Another participant stated, 'attending open evenings and parents' evenings just reminds me that school wasn't for me, and I understand it probably isn't for my kid either because they (the teachers) aren't like us and don't understand us'. This is reflected throughout the interviews from the study, particularly resonating through the UK-born parents and in the immigrant parents where they felt alienated from the local community. The frustrations of the participants can be linked to the aims of the government as discussed by Goodman and Burton (2012), who observed that the push to raise pupil standards does not resolve inequalities in education and the local community, and when they look at the progress of pupils, the government measures their grades over community engagement or aspirations for non-academic careers.

The case study found that the engagement of parents was, in their own view, passive rather than active, and that when they did engage, only one parent would attend parents' evenings, often the mother rather than the father, with it being because of an expectation rather than a desire to attend. One participant from a UK-born family stated, 'the formal feeling in the school and the judgement of my role as a dad, makes me feel defensive, it doesn't make me feel like we are on the same side'. Further to this, another participant explained, 'if the events are just to tell me what I am doing wrong, then what is the point of it, they want me to motivate my children, but they don't motivate me to want to do that'. The range of reasons discovered within the study included not being able to access the information shared by teachers comfortably and feeling that they were not respected by the educational community; also, that they had not been comfortable at school themselves and still found that a barrier.

Within the case study, a comparison of UK-born and immigrant families was made, and the importance of parental engagement was found to be a key role from the perceptions of the immigrant parents. The unique position of the immigrant families was found to be a motivator for pushing their children to engage and achieve throughout all key stages and to be driven to develop aspirations for their transitions throughout their education. Immigrant parents, defined in the study as first-generation immigrant parents of children in attendance at the case study school, are shown in the research to want their children to use their education as an opportunity to improve their life and ensure they can establish a successful future for themselves. One of the parents who participated in the study explained, 'I want to attend events and help the teachers as much as I can to do their job, we have travelled and settled here so that we can build a future, and I know that school can help my daughter do that.' This response was a common theme throughout the immigrant participants in the study and one participant compared their attitude with UK-born parents, stating, 'I feel like it is not right to complain about the school, if you are not supporting the teachers to do their job, it takes more than just a teacher or a parent to get a child to get the best out of school.' The children in turn are aware of the opportunities their parents have provided them with through their immigration and feel a responsibility to repay their families through their engagement. Kao and Tienda (2022) support this suggestion, surmising that immigrant parents do have high expectations for their children in academia and that their children understand and agree with this aspiration. The immigrant parents felt it was equally their role to be engaged with the education of their children and that they must support teachers by monitoring home learning and behaviour.

The case study found that the disillusionment of the parents from working-class UK-born families was linked to their own experiences of education and had led them to avoid attendance at parent meetings and to feel that they had little to offer in assisting their child in transitions and choices within the education system. They felt that where their own academic journey had failed, they had managed to make a career without these academic successes and therefore they did not see the relevance of promoting this with their own child. Stopforth and colleagues (2024) further support this, stating that social class is directly linked to the engagement of children and their parents in education while acknowledging some ethnic groups and immigrant families are at odds with this theory regardless of their socio-economic status.

Suggestions from the parents involved in the study to build engagement are listed below.

1. Provide courses and events at accessible times to teach new styles of learning for them to feel empowered to help their children engage.
2. Where language is a barrier for immigrant parents, offering access to basic English to help support their children.

3. Give parents the opportunity to access information on courses in advance of discussions with their child so that they can feel informed and confident in discussing these choices with them.
4. Make sure that positive communication is made as important as negative communication so that it feels like parents and teachers are working together for the child.
5. Listen to parent feedback on what they need to encourage them to engage with events and transition points.
6. Celebrate working-class roles as well as those that require further and higher education.

Key takeaways:

- Immigrant families would like to gain support to access English lessons to enable them to accurately help their children, where they cannot already speak English.
- Working-class parents feel overlooked by the current education system.
- To engage parents, schools need to build open and honest lines of communication that involve acting on parent voice.

Implications for teaching and leadership staff

The challenges of building lines of communication in the local community for school is not just about having a shared interest in the education of the young people attending the school. The challenges include overcoming barriers with effective communication where language or cultural differences provide a barrier but also in overcoming the challenges faced in the disadvantaged areas of the community. To enable this to improve, school leaders and teachers need to build strength in triangulation of communication between all stakeholders. Skaliotis (2010) outlined that the challenge of secondary transitions is linked to the decline in parental engagement and particularly where there are behaviours that the school request support with. This decline in involvement is reflected with a rise in there often being only one parent maintaining the relationship with the school.

Opportunities to maximize relationships with parents to ensure inclusive transitions can be developed during initial contact at open evenings when parents are looking to select the school and in selecting next steps for post-16.

The opportunity to then build on these relationships during parents' evenings and regular contact through information shared with home and invitations to celebrate progress towards future transition processes is key to ensure that the relationships that are established in primary school can continue into secondary school. Kiuru and colleagues (2020) suggest that the relationships established during the beginning of the working relationships between teachers or leadership staff and the parents can allow key information to be shared and expectations to be agreed that start the journey for their child with a solid foundation and a shared consensus on how to support the transition points.

The following advice may help to maintain and build on these relationships to strengthen transition points.

1. Maintaining dialogue and not a one-way street between educators and parents will break down the barrier.
2. Listening to the expert knowledge that the parent can share and acknowledging the strength of that input.
3. Celebrating all careers when looking at options with children, making sure that the wider community is celebrated.

Further reading

Further research to look at the changing face of challenges faced in secondary school transitions and the rising absenteeism and its impact on parental engagement in education can provide further insight.

Publications that may be a good start are:

MacDonald, R., & Marsh, J. (2004) Missing school: Educational engagement, youth transitions, and social exclusion. *Youth & Society*, 36(2), 143–62.

Martin, J., Bowl, M., & Banks, G. (eds.) (2023) *Mapping the Field: 75 Years of Educational Review*. Volume II. 1st ed. Abingdon: Routledge. https://doi.org/10.4324/9781003403722.

References

Anderson, K.P. (2020) Academic, attendance, and behavioral outcomes of a suspension reduction policy: Lessons for school leaders and policy makers. *Educational Administration Quarterly*, 56(3), 435–71.

Ariani, F., Ulfatin, N., Supriyanto, A., & Arifin, I. (2022) Implementing online integrated character education and parental engagement in local cultural values cultivation. *European Journal of Educational Research*, *11*(3), 1699–714.

Bagnall, C.L., Skipper, Y., & Fox, C.L. (2020) 'You're in this world now': Students', teachers', and parents' experiences of school transition and how they feel it can be improved. *British Journal of Educational Psychology*, *90*(1), 206–26.

Brown, P., & Souto-Otero, M. (2020). The end of the credential society? An analysis of the relationship between education and the labour market using big data. *Journal of Education Policy*, *35*(1), 95–118.

Carter, B. (2017) *Engaging Parents in Their Children's Education*. K4D Helpdesk Report. Brighton: Institute of Development Studies.

Department for Education (2017) Engaging parents and families. Can be found online at Engaging parents and families (publishing.service.gov.uk).

Department for Education (2024) Using pupil premium: Guidance for school leaders. Can be found online at Using Pupil Premium: Guidance for School Leaders (publishing.service.gov.uk).

Education Endowment Foundation (2021) Working with parents to support children's learning. Available from: https://d2tic4wvo1iusb.cloudfront.net/production/eef-guidance-reports/supporting-parents/EEF_Parental_Engagement_Guidance_Report.pdf?v=1748082140.

Education Endowment Foundation (2024) Parental engagement. Can be found online at Parental engagement | EEF (educationendowmentfoundation.org.uk).

Explore Education Statistics (2024) Suspensions and permanent exclusions in England. Can be found online at Suspensions and permanent exclusions in England, Academic year 2022/23 – Explore education statistics – GOV.UK (explore-education-statistics.service.gov.uk).

Goetz, T., Bieleke, M., Gogol, K., van Tartwijk, J., Mainhard, T., Lipnevich, A.A., & Pekrun, R. (2021) Getting along and feeling good: Reciprocal associations between student-teacher relationship quality and students' emotions. *Learning and Instruction*, *71*, 101349.

Goodman, R., & Burton, D. (2012) What is the nature of the achievement gap, why does it persist and are government goals sufficient to create social justice in the education system? *Education 3-13*, *40*(5), 500–14.

Green, F. (2020) Schoolwork in lockdown: New evidence on the epidemic of educational poverty. Centre for Learning and Life Chances in Knowledge Economies and Societies (LLAkes). Available from: https://www.llakes.ac.uk/sites/default/files/LLAKES%20Working%20Paper%2067_0.pdf.

Hornby, G., & Lafaele, R. (2011) Barriers to parental involvement in education: An explanatory model. *Educational Review*, *63*(1), 37–52.

Jerrim, J. (2023) Test anxiety: Is it associated with performance in high-stakes examinations? *Oxford Review of Education*, *49*(3), 321–41.

Kao, G., & Tienda, M. (2022) Optimism and achievement: The educational performance of immigrant youth. In: Suárez-Orozoco, M.M., Suárez-Orozoco, C., and Qin-Hilliard, D. (eds.), *The New Immigrants and American Schools* (pp. 83–101). Routledge. https://doi.org/10.4324/9781315054216-4.

Kiuru, N., Wang, M.T., Salmela-Aro, K., Kannas, L., Ahonen, T., & Hirvonen, R. (2020) Associations between adolescents' interpersonal relationships, school well-being, and academic achievement during educational transitions. *Journal of Youth and Adolescence, 49*(5), 1057–72.

Pollard, A., Daly, C., Burn, K., Higgins, S., Kennedy, A., Mulholland, M., & Yandell, J. (2023) *Reflective Teaching in Secondary Schools*. 6th ed. London: Bloomsbury Academic.

Posey-Maddox, L., & Haley-Lock, A. (2020) One size does not fit all: Understanding parent engagement in the contexts of work, family, and public schooling. *Urban Education, 55*(5), 671–98.

Reay, D. (2008) Tony Blair, the promotion of the 'active' educational citizen, and middle-class hegemony. *Oxford Review of Education, 34*(6), 639–50. Can be found online at Using Pupil Premium: Guidance for School Leaders (publishing.service. gov.uk).

Skaliotis, E. (2010) Changes in parental involvement in secondary education: An exploration study using the longitudinal study of young people in England. *British Educational Research Journal, 36*(6), 975–94.

Smyth, E. (2020) Shaping educational expectations: The perspectives of 13-year-olds and their parents. *Educational Review, 72*(2), 173–95.

Stopforth, S., Connelly, R., & Gayle, V. (2024) Do you like school? Social class, gender, ethnicity and pupils' educational enjoyment. *The British Journal of Sociology, 75*(4), 535–53.

Wilkinson, C. (Pending) Parental perception of the importance of their engagement in their child's education.

8

Behaviour and Integration into School Culture

Karl Rogerson

Overview of chapter

Pupil behaviour in schools has a significant impact on both academic and social outcomes. When behaviour improves, pupils achieve more, learning time is better used, and staff are happier, leading to better retention and recruitment. However, many schools still struggle with managing behaviour, where leadership plays such a crucial role. While teachers are essential, they can only do so much without strong, consistent support from school leaders.

Thus, the challenge for school leaders is establishing and sustaining a positive school culture – essentially defining 'the way we do things here' – that everyone in the school community understands and follows. This chapter examines various aspects of pupils' behaviour, including the critical transitions between educational settings and how they relate to school culture. It shows how these elements shape the educational experiences in both primary and secondary schools. Whilst doing this, it recognizes the uniqueness of each school and classroom and gives evidence-based strategies that can be adapted to support this mission.

Much has been written about school culture, for example, Gruenert and Whitaker (2015), *School Culture Rewired: How to Define, Assess, and Transform it* and Fullan's (2007) 'The New Meaning of Educational Change'.

In simple terms, it can be described as a mix of the norms, values, and practices everyone shares in the school. The chapter explores how behaviour-management strategies and efforts to integrate different cultures can help or hinder pupils' academic and social growth, especially during transitions. Drawing from my own experience as a school leader and Research School Director, the chapter examines how individual behaviour connects to the broader school culture.

A case study from. a multicultural primary school in a high-deprivation area illustrates the everyday experiences of pupils, teachers and staff, providing a real-world look at what works and what does not. By analysing recent educational research, the chapter supports a well-rounded approach to behaviour management, focusing on inclusivity, positive relationships and consistency. It emphasizes the need for a supportive school environment to achieve positive outcomes and provides practical strategies to help enhance school culture.

Current policy/contexts

Over the past twenty years, the policy and context of behaviour in English schools have undergone significant changes, shaped by evolving educational priorities, government interventions, societal changes and of course, the Covid-19 pandemic. Transitions between different educational settings have also increasingly been recognized as critical points affecting pupil behaviour.

During this period, several key publications have helped shape schools' approaches to managing and supporting behaviour. In 2003, the government published 'Every Child Matters' (DfES, 2003), focusing on promoting the wellbeing of children from birth to age nineteen, covering health, safety, and achieving potential. This was the starting point for a more holistic approach to behaviour, recognizing emotional and social factors that impact behaviour at home and school. Further to this, 'Mental Health and Behaviour in Schools' (Department for Education, 2014) highlighted the impact of mental health on behaviour, encouraging schools to integrate mental health support into behaviour policies. Building on the work developed following 'Every Child Matters', it offers advice on supporting pupils with mental health needs and how this impacts their behaviour, including during transitions.

In 2005, the Department for Education and Skills (2005), Learning behaviour: The report of the Practitioners' Group on School Behaviour and Discipline – also known as The Steer Report – provided recommendations on managing behaviour in schools, advocating for a structured, consistent approach – something I will revisit throughout this chapter. The report emphasized that 'there is no single solution to the problem of poor behaviour, but all schools have the potential to raise standards if they are consistent in implementing good practice in learning, teaching, and behaviour management' (DfES, 2005, p. 7). This highlights the need for skilful and careful adaptation to context, including managing transitions effectively.

Additionally, in 2011, the Department for Education published *Behaviour and Discipline in Schools: A Guide for Headteachers and School Staff* (DfE, 2011). This guidance provides a framework for school leaders and teachers on how to manage behaviour and discipline, including advice on creating behaviour policies, the use of rewards and sanctions and legal powers related to discipline. This document – updated regularly – guides the day-to-day behaviour management in schools, reflecting the shift towards more consistent, structured and legally informed approaches.

Finally, the Education Endowment Foundation's (2019) report, Improving Behaviour in Schools, became particularly relevant following the Covid-19 pandemic. It offers six evidence-based recommendations to improve school behaviour, including understanding pupils and their influences, teaching-learning behaviours and maintaining consistency.

It is worth noting that there are many other publications and articles exploring school-level behaviour – please refer to the further reading section at the end of this chapter for more information. What I have highlighted here are key documents significant in shaping how school leaders develop behaviour culture, particularly around transition points.

Key takeaways:

- Behaviour policies should adopt a holistic approach, addressing emotional and social factors
- Mental health support should be integrated into behaviour management, especially during transitions
- Consistency and evidence-based practices are key to improving behaviour, particularly post-Covid-19.

Academic changes and curriculum requirements

In England, the national curriculum does not explicitly mandate behaviour management strategies, but it does state expectations that support positive behaviour through its design and teaching. There is an expectation that schools create environments that foster good behaviour as it is essential for high-quality learning and personal development.

Although Personal, Social, Health and Economic (PSHE) education is a non-statutory subject, it is crucial during school transitions because it equips pupils with the emotional, social and mental health skills needed to manage change. It helps them develop resilience, emotional literacy and coping strategies, all of which are vital when navigating transitions like moving between key stages or schools.

Evidence from the Education Endowment Foundation (EEF)'s *Metacognition and Self-Regulated Learning Guidance Report* (2018) supports the theory that teachers should also integrate learning behaviours like resilience, self-regulation and perseverance into the curriculum, moving beyond merely managing misbehaviour. Teaching these skills helps pupils develop a proactive mindset towards learning and challenges, fostering independence and problem-solving abilities. Further embedding these behaviours enables pupils to respond constructively to setbacks, particularly during transitional periods, where uncertainty and new expectations can affect behaviour.

By teaching pupils how to manage their emotions and persevere through difficulties, teachers and leaders can create a culture where positive behaviour is sustained through self-motivation. This holistic approach empowers pupils to take ownership of their actions, improving both academic and behavioural outcomes.

Key takeaway:

- Integrating PSHE into the curriculum supports pupils during transitions, improving academic and behavioural outcomes.

Social/relational changes

Research, such as, Scottish Government (2017), *Primary-secondary transitions: A systematic literature review,* suggests transitioning between educational settings, such as primary to secondary school, involves significant social and relational changes that can impact pupil behaviour. These changes often influence how pupils interact with their peers and teachers and how they settle into and navigate this new environment. Here are some key social and relational changes that affect behaviour during these transitions:

Changes in social dynamics

Pupils often find themselves in larger, more diverse peer groups. The need to form new friendships and find a place within these groups can create social anxiety and affect behaviour. Pupils may exhibit behaviours aimed at fitting in, such as adopting new attitudes or engaging in behaviours they believe will make them more accepted by their peers. The desire to be accepted by new peers can lead to increased susceptibility to peer pressure and manifest in both positive and negative behaviours, depending on the norms of the new peer group.

Changes in teacher-pupil relationships

In primary school, pupils often have close, supportive relationships with a small number of teachers and teaching assistants who they have built a strong relationship with over time. However, in secondary school, pupils interact with many teachers, each responsible for different subjects. This can result in pupils feeling less individually known and supported, potentially leading to misunderstandings about behaviour and what is triggering such behaviours.

To pupils and parents, it can also feel like secondary schools have higher expectations for pupils' independence and responsibility. The shift from the nurturing environment of primary school to the more structured and demanding environment of secondary school can cause some pupils – particularly the most vulnerable – to struggle with the adjustment, leading to behavioural issues as they try to understand and adapt to new expectations.

The Establish-Maintain-Restore (EMR) method (Cook et al., 2017) is a practical framework that focuses on building positive relationships with pupils and can be particularly useful at points of transition. It is designed to help teachers build, sustain, and repair relationships with pupils, particularly those who may struggle with behaviour or engagement. Here's how the method works across its three phases:

1. Establish:
   This step focuses on intentionally building a positive relationship with the pupil from the start. This involves getting to know the pupil and showing interest in their life and interests.
   The aim here is to create a foundation of trust and mutual respect.
2. Maintain:
   Once the relationship has been established, it needs to be nurtured over time, by reinforcing positive interactions, providing support and recognizing efforts and progress.
   Here it is about keeping the relationship strong by being attentive. Maintaining relationships can help prevent disengagement because pupils are more likely to respond positively to a teacher they feel connected with.

3. Restore:

   Despite these efforts, misbehaviour may still occur. This phase focuses on repairing the relationship after it has been strained or broken, due to a behavioural issue. Acknowledging the problem, offering an opportunity for reconciliation, and working collaboratively to rebuild the trust that was lost is essential. Restoring relationships is crucial for maintaining a positive classroom environment and ensuring pupils feel supported, even more so after a conflict.

Although it may seem time-consuming, the effort invested in his approach can yield significant benefits in promoting a positive learning environment and can be achieved in short, regular intervals. I must stress that there is no 'magic wand' here! It takes commitment from the individual teacher and a whole school approach, but I have personally seen the benefits of this approach when implemented consistently.

Studies (for example, EEF, 2019) have also shown that the use of report cards, or 'check in' cards as I prefer to call them, can be effective in supporting pupils with challenging behaviour. They can, but the crucial point is who they report to – particularly those pupils who are new to school. Is it someone they trust or have a positive relationship with? This is essential as the time spent with this individual should be spent exploring positive and negative behaviour in a safe space and at a safe time. This is particularly important for pupils who are transitioning to a new school – particularly those moving in year. Schools can do this effectively by identifying a key adult to meet and greet the pupil and family and maintaining this relationship as the pupil moves through school.

As part of his work as a special adviser to the government, Charlie Taylor (Taylor, 2011) developed a behaviour checklist that highlights actions for teachers and headteachers, so let's explore some of those recommendations here.

Classroom

Meet and greet pupils when they come into the classroom. This sets a positive tone from the start of the lesson/day. It helps develop a sense of belonging and strengthens the teacher-pupil relationship. School leaders can utilize the same approach at the school gate.

Display rules in the class and ensure that the pupils and staff know what they are – particularly relevant for pupils transitioning to a new-year group, school or learning environment. Displaying the rules, referring to them regularly and explaining why we have them reinforce accountability and fairness and ensure consequences are consistent for all.

Have a system in place to follow through with all sanctions and a system in place to follow through with all rewards – consistency is key in both areas and pupils will remind teachers about this if they are not applied fairly. As a teacher and leader, it is of paramount importance to support a positive culture of learning. When sanctions and rewards are not followed through, the culture of positive behaviour will quickly fall apart – and take a long time to re-establish. Trust needs to be earned by all adults.

Pupils

Teachers should praise the behaviour they want to see more of and praise children doing the right thing more than criticizing those who are doing the wrong thing. This encourages desirable behaviours. Shifting the focus towards constructive behaviour rather than destructive teachers and leaders creates a climate for learning for all. Pupils new to a school will quickly fit into this positive culture.

Ensure that all resources are prepared in advance – it seems so simple but can be a challenge in the busy day of a teacher, particularly an inexperienced one. Having resources prepared reduces 'downtime' which can often be a trigger for restless and fidgety behaviour which can quickly escalate. Being prepared means the teacher can focus on those pupils who may need extra guidance and support to engage in the learning, particularly at the beginning of lessons, whilst enabling the rest of the class to work independently.

Teacher and parent relationships

Give feedback to parents about their child's behaviour and let them know about the good days as well as the bad ones – it can be too easy to make the first interaction with parents a negative one when reporting poor behaviour. Effective practice is when school leaders and teachers take every opportunity to communicate the positive moments in a pupil's life. This helps build trust and supports ongoing support from home.

Individual responsibility for learning

As pupils move on to secondary and primary education, they are often given more autonomy, such as managing their timetable, organizing homework and navigating larger school environments. This increase in responsibility can be overwhelming for some pupils, leading to stress and potential behaviour changes.

Key takeaways:

- Social dynamics: Larger peer groups can increase social anxiety and peer pressure.
- Teacher relationships: Pupils interact with more teachers, potentially feeling less supported, and leading to potential behaviour issues.
- Responsibility: Greater independence in managing schedules can overwhelm pupils, causing stress and behaviour changes.

Assessment

Regular formative assessment (ongoing, informal checks for understanding) helps leaders and teachers identify behavioural patterns related to learning difficulties. For example, a pupil's disruptive behaviour might stem from struggles with a specific subject or concept, and tailored interventions can address both academic and behavioural issues. This is an area that can often be overlooked, particularly at transition points in a pupil's life.

Providing constructive feedback based on these assessments, and identifying strengths and areas for development, can foster positive behaviour and a 'can do' approach. When pupils understand what they need to improve and are given support to do so, their engagement and self-regulation tend to increase. Behaviour improves when pupils feel that they are progressing and capable of meeting learning goals. Of course, this will not happen instantly and should be seen as a method of identifying short-term goals to effect a positive change in long-term behaviour.

Do not underestimate the importance of challenging pupils to achieve their potential. When pupils perceive a lack of challenge in their learning, they can quickly become bored and restless. The same can apply when work presented to pupils is not matched correctly to their ability and they are unable to access the work. Misdiagnosis of a pupil's ability and lack of challenge can have a significant effect on pupils' engagement in learning as can work that is not accessible to pupils. This emphasizes the importance of accurate summative assessment and regular formative assessment in the classroom. As a result of accurate assessment, skilful adaptations to practice can be woven into sequences of learning to enable all pupils to experience challenge and success, therefore supporting their engagement and achievement.

An essential part of ongoing formative assessment is carefully crafted feedback. This feedback, when delivered effectively, should focus on task, subject and self-regulation. As Wiliam (2017) states in much of his work on embedding formative assessment, 'feedback should cause thinking'. Therefore, it is vital to invest time at transition points to achieve an accurate representation of a pupil's ability so that the curriculum they experience is appropriate for their learning needs and potential misconceptions are mitigated. Formative feedback and assessment is a high-leverage strategy that should be integrated across all areas of school life. When delivered consistently, it should form a key component of a positive learning experience.

Key takeaways:

- Formative assessment addresses learning and behaviour: Ongoing assessments help identify academic challenges that may influence behaviour, allowing for targeted support.
- Constructive feedback boosts engagement: Clear, actionable feedback encourages pupils, supporting positive learning behaviours and self-regulation when matched to their ability.

Impact of place

Exposure to a different school culture

Each educational setting has its own culture and set of social norms. Pupils transitioning to a new school must quickly learn and adapt to these new expectations, which can be challenging. Behavioural issues may arise as pupils test the boundaries of what is acceptable in their new environment or as they struggle to understand the 'culture' within the school.

An over-reliance on 'what' the rules are rather than understanding 'why' we have these rules can result in a culture of resentment towards such rules, further enhancing a lack of belonging. Initial findings from ImpactED (2024) show that pupils' sense of belonging at school has a statistically significant impact on their attendance rates. Prior research has also demonstrated that a strong sense of school belonging is linked to increased student motivation, reductions in absenteeism and improved academic achievement (Riley et al., 2020).

Alongside this, pupils can often encounter peers from a wider range of backgrounds and experiences. This increased diversity can lead to richer, positive social interactions but can also cause conflicts or misunderstandings, especially if pupils lack the skills to navigate these differences. A school culture and curriculum that proactively recognizes these potential conflicts can address many of these issues before they occur and support successful reconciliation.

Emotional responses to change

The uncertainty of a new environment can lead to anxiety, which may manifest as behavioural changes such as withdrawal, aggression or avoidance. Pupils may struggle with the loss of familiar routines and relationships, and this emotional turbulence – often heightened by puberty – can impact their behaviour in and outside the classroom. Unfamiliar faces, spaces, routines and expectations can be particularly challenging for pupils who are sensitive to change – such as those with special educational needs, leading to feelings of insecurity, which might result in withdrawal, or acting out as they seek to regain a sense of control.

Online behaviour

The transition period can also affect online behaviour. Research indicates that children's online activity increases as they transition to secondary school. A 2024 report by Ofcom found that 90 per cent of children own a mobile phone by age eleven, facilitating greater internet access. Pupils will often increase their use of social media as they continue to develop their independence. This may help to navigate their new social environment, but adversely it may sometimes result in cyberbullying, peer pressure or the development of unhealthy online habits that can influence their in-school behaviour.

> **Key takeaways:**
>
> - School culture: Adapting to new social norms can challenge pupils, leading to behavioural issues, especially if they don't feel a sense of belonging, which can impact attendance and motivation.
> - Emotional responses: Anxiety from unfamiliar environments can manifest as withdrawal or aggression, particularly in vulnerable pupils.
> - Online behaviour: Increased social media use can lead to cyberbullying, peer pressure or unhealthy habits affecting in-school behaviour.

Case study

'Transforming school culture and behaviour at Billwed Academy' (anonymized)

Background:

Billwed Academy, located in the West Midlands, faced significant challenges related to poor student behaviour, low academic performance and negative school culture. In 2010, the school was placed in special measures by Ofsted due to these issues. The school needed fundamental change in both behaviour management and overall school culture.

To address these challenges, Billwed Academy implemented a strategic plan centred on transforming the school's culture and improving pupils' behaviour. Key strategies included:

1. Leadership change: A new headteacher and deputy headteacher were appointed, bringing a clear vision for change and a strong focus on high expectations for both pupils and staff.
2. Clear and consistent behaviour policies: The school introduced a rigorous and clearly defined behaviour policy that set high expectations for pupils' behaviour. This policy was consistently enforced across all year groups, ensuring that all pupils understood the consequences of their actions, but more importantly that all adults understood their responsibilities in ensuring fairness and consistency.
3. Focus on routines and structure: Daily routines were established to create a structured environment. This included the introduction of a simple

uniform policy and standardized classroom procedures. The goal was to minimize distractions and create a calm, orderly environment conducive to learning.

4. An emphasis on positive relationships: Alongside the simple but structured policies, the school implemented a culture where everyone had a voice. Everyone was aware of their rights but more importantly, their responsibility towards all members of the school community. This approach emphasized repairing harm and rebuilding relationships when behavioural issues occurred, promoting a sense of responsibility and community for pupils, staff and parents.
5. Data-driven decision making: Regularly monitoring behaviour data helped leaders identify trends, address issues promptly and adjust strategies as needed.
6. Professional development for staff: The school invested heavily in training for teachers and support staff, focusing on classroom management techniques, high-quality teaching, relationship building and the consistent application of the new behaviour policies. This involved establishing support structures for teachers, such as mentoring and peer collaboration.
7. Curriculum: The curriculum was designed to highlight the cultural diversity of the school population, engage pupils and contribute to their positive behaviour and enthusiasm for learning. The school's approach ensured that behaviour management and curriculum delivery were integrated, promoting a supportive and productive learning environment.
8. Parental engagement: Billwed also worked to strengthen relationships with parents, involving them in the school's efforts to improve behaviour and culture. Regular meetings, workshops and clear communication were key elements of this strategy.

Impact

The comprehensive approach taken by Billwed led to significant improvements in both behaviour and overall school culture over this initial twelve-month period. However, it is important to recognize that to sustain and develop this culture, skilful adaptations are required over time. The school achieved an Ofsted grade of outstanding in 2017 in recognition of this.

- Improved behaviour: There was a marked reduction in behavioural incidents, with fewer pupils receiving sanctions or being excluded from

school. The structured routines contributed to a more focused and disciplined learning environment.
- Positive school culture: The school culture shifted dramatically, with a greater sense of pride and belonging among pupils, parents and staff. The emphasis on high expectations and consistency helped to foster a positive, respectful atmosphere throughout the school.
- Academic improvement: Alongside improvements in behaviour and culture, the school saw a corresponding rise in academic performance. Pupils became more engaged in their learning, contributing to better outcomes across various subjects.
- Enhanced teacher morale: Teachers reported feeling more supported and empowered to manage classrooms effectively, leading to increased job satisfaction, retention and career progression.

Conclusion

Billwed's transformation highlights the critical importance of strong leadership, consistent behaviour policies, an ambitious curriculum offer and relationships in creating a positive school culture. These elements are crucial during key transitions in education, such as moving from primary to secondary school or transitioning between year groups. Managing these transitions effectively can prevent disruptions in behaviour and ensure that pupils adapt smoothly to new environments.

The school's success demonstrates that with the right strategies, even schools facing significant challenges can turn around behaviour and culture, leading to better outcomes for pupils and staff alike. Ensuring continuity and support during transitions helps maintain the positive progress made within a school's culture and discipline.

> **Key takeaways:**
>
> - Leadership change: Strong leadership with a clear vision was critical. New leadership implemented high expectations and drove the school's cultural shift.
> - Consistent behaviour policies: Clear, consistently applied behaviour policies helped establish a structured and disciplined learning environment.
> - Focus on relationships: Emphasizing positive relationships and community responsibility was central to the school's approach to behaviour management.
> - Ambitious curriculum: The curriculum was designed to reflect cultural diversity, engage pupils and integrate behaviour management, contributing to improved academic outcomes.

Implications for teachers and leaders

Understanding that pupils may exhibit poor behaviour both in and out of the classroom is a challenge for teachers. The key lies in identifying strategies that effectively promote positive behaviour and manage disruptive behaviour. The EEF Guidance Report Improving Behaviour in Schools (2019) draws from a range of international research and input from educators to provide actionable insights. It suggests that teachers should take a thoughtful and structured approach, so let's look at this in more detail.

Implications for teachers

Recommendation 1: Know and understand your pupils and their influences

Implication: When pupils trust their teachers, they are more open to support, and teachers can address the underlying causes of behavioural issues more effectively.

Strategy: Spend time getting to know pupils beyond surface-level interactions and use trust as a tool to understand the causes of misbehaviour and tailor support accordingly.

Recommendation 2: Teach learning behaviours alongside managing misbehaviour

Implication: Effective behaviour management is not just employing strategies for when pupils misbehave. As Ellis and Tod (2014) emphasize, 'The successful management of behaviour relies on far more than a set of strategies to draw upon when pupils misbehave' (p. 8). Instead, it involves teaching pupils how to respond appropriately to challenges.

Strategy: Explicitly teach and model learning behaviours like resilience, teamwork and self-regulation. Move from control to teaching: Focus on learning behaviours rather than merely enforcing rules.

Recommendation 3: Use classroom management strategies to support good classroom behaviour

Implication: Evidence shows that poor classroom behaviour significantly impacts pupil learning. OFSTED's Below the Radar (2014) report highlights that up to an hour of learning per day may be lost to low-level disruption. Since the Covid-19 pandemic, teachers have reported an increase in incidents of poor behaviour. This reinforces the need for clear, consistent rules and routines to maintain a positive learning environment.

Strategy: Create and maintain consistent behavioural expectations, communicated at the start of the year and reinforced regularly. Balance between positive reinforcement and appropriate sanctions is key to fostering a productive classroom culture.

Use evidence-based programmes: Implement frameworks like 'The Incredible Years Teacher Classroom Management Training' (Webster-Stratton & Reid, 2010), which focus on strengthening classroom management, promoting positive behaviour and reducing disruption.

Recommendation 4: Use simple approaches as part of your regular routine

Implication: Classroom routines and strategies like regular check-ins, greeting pupils at the door, using visual cues and ensuring smooth transitions between activities are essential for promoting positive behaviour. Consistency is crucial in applying these strategies, helping them understand expectations and ensuring fairness.

Strategy: Implement consistent routines: Regularly check in with pupils, use visual cues and create predictable transitions to maintain structure. Apply these strategies uniformly to promote fairness and reinforce clear expectations.

Recommendation 5: Use targeted approaches to meet the needs of individuals in your school

Implication: While consistency in rules is essential for classroom management, flexibility is also necessary, especially for pupils with specific behavioural challenges. This can seem contradictory, as flexibility might be perceived as allowing certain pupils to avoid accountability. However, individualized strategies that cater to unique needs are vital, reinforcing the whole school behaviour policy while maintaining fairness.

Strategy: Develop individual strategies by collaborating with staff. Use behaviour-tracking data and transitional data to create tailored interventions for pupils with specific challenges. Utilize nonverbal cues: Employ subtle techniques such as proximity (moving closer to off-task pupils), engagement prompts (asking relevant questions) and offering choices to redirect behaviour without disrupting the lesson.

Recommendation 6: Consistency is key

Implication: Classroom-level strategies significantly influence pupil behaviour, and while relationships and consistency are crucial, a whole school approach to behaviour management is essential for long-term effectiveness.

Strategy: Ensure consistency: Consistently apply the behaviour policy, ensuring rules and rewards for positive behaviour are uniformly enforced. Collaborate with colleagues: Work together with colleagues to implement behaviour policies consistently across the school, helping pupils understand that expectations remain the same in different settings and classes.

Implications for leadership

The responsibility of school leaders is to integrate an approach to behaviour that is embedded in the culture of the school. This approach will require careful creation, adaptation and implementation as it must be embedded in all areas of school life and understood by all members of the school community.

Bennett (2017) has highlighted commonly found features in successful schools. These features include:

- committed, highly visible school leaders, with ambitious goals, supported by a strong leadership team;
- effectively communicated, realistic, detailed expectations understood clearly by all members of the school;
- highly consistent working practices throughout the school;
- a clear understanding of what the school culture is 'this is how we do things around here, and these are the values we hold';
- high levels of staff and parental commitment to the school vision and strategies;
- high levels of support between leadership and staff, for example, staff training;

- attention to detail and thoroughness in the execution of school policies and strategies; and
- high expectations of all pupils and staff and a belief that all pupils matter equally.

These resources serve as valuable starting points for senior leadership teams to assess their school's current standing. It is important to note that Tom Bennett's ideas and approach, as well as the EEF recommendations, are contested by some in the education profession. The recommendations are based on specific evidence from a broad base but may not necessarily be suitable for every context. The key is knowing your context and using your knowledge and skills to apply these principles to your school or setting.

Below I have suggested some specific strategies that school leaders can implement to influence the culture of behaviour within their schools, aligning with the key recommendations from the Education Endowment Foundation (2019):

Recommendation 1: Know and understand your pupils and their influences

Implication: Leaders must create systems for gathering and analysing pupils' background information to tailor support effectively. This is especially important for the most vulnerable pupils, including those with SEND.

Strategy: Implement cross-phase systems and regular staff training on pupil backgrounds.

Recommendation 2: Teach learning behaviours alongside managing misbehaviour

Implication: There needs to be a shift in focus from purely reactive measures to proactive teaching of positive behaviours. Find out what your partner schools are doing.

Strategy: Incorporate social-emotional learning (SEL) into the curriculum and provide teachers with tools for embedding behaviour management within lessons.

Recommendation 3: Use classroom management strategies to support good classroom behaviour

Implication: Consistent, school-wide classroom management techniques must be adopted and monitored.

Strategy: Establish a behaviour management policy – developed with all stakeholders, including feeder schools – that includes clear expectations and regular teacher professional development to ensure effective implementation.

Recommendation 4: Use simple approaches as part of your regular routine

Implication: Leaders must ensure that simple, effective behaviour strategies are embedded into daily routines.

Strategy: Introduce school-wide routines such as greeting pupils at the door and school gate, retrieval activities at the start of lessons and regular acknowledgement of positive behaviour. Monitor their implementation!

Recommendation 5: Use targeted approaches to meet the needs of individuals in your school

Implication: Tailored interventions require resources and time, which necessitates careful planning and allocation.

Strategy: Develop individualized behaviour plans for pupils with persistent issues, supported by regular monitoring and making adjustments. Meet regularly with parents to review these approaches. As a leader, model these approaches, and take time to explain why they are necessary.

Recommendation 6: Consistency is key

Implication: Consistency across the entire school community is essential but challenging to maintain.

Strategy: Foster a shared understanding of behaviour policies through continuous professional development, consistent communication, especially at key transition points, and strong leadership commitment to the policies.

For successful implementation, school leaders must focus on professional development, clear communication and monitoring of behaviour strategies to ensure they are embedded into the culture of the school and consistently applied. This will not only support pupils at key transition points in their educational life but it will also support all pupils to achieve their full potential and feel happy and safe in school.

Further reading and support

- **Department for Education (2014) Below the Radar: Low-Level Disruption in the Country's Classrooms**
  This report provides insights into the prevalence and impact of low-level disruption in classrooms across England. Understanding these disruptions is crucial for developing effective strategies to manage and reduce them.

- **Dix, P. (2017)** *When the Adults Change, Everything Changes: Seismic Shifts in School Behaviour.* **Carmarthen: Independent Thinking Press.**

Paul Dix's book focuses on how changing adult behaviour and attitudes can lead to significant improvements in school behaviour. It emphasizes the role of all adults in school in modelling positive behaviour and setting a culture of respect and high expectations.

- **Education Endowment Foundation (2019) Improving Social and Emotional Learning in Primary Schools**
This guidance report provides evidence-based recommendations for enhancing social and emotional learning (SEL) in primary schools. The report offers practical advice on integrating SEL into the curriculum and fostering a supportive learning environment. Application to context is key!

References

Bennett, T. (2017) Creating a culture: How school leaders can optimise behaviour. Department for Education. Available from: https://assets.publishing.service.gov.uk/media/5a7506e4ed915d3c7d529cec/Tom_Bennett_Independent_Review_of_Behaviour_in_Schools.pdf.

Cook, C.R., Miller, F.G., Fiat, A., Renshaw, T., Frye, M., Joseph, G. and Decano, P. (2017), Promoting secondary teachers' well-being and intentions to implement evidence-based practices: randomized evaluation of the achiever resilience curriculum. *Psychol. Schs.*, 54: 13–28. https://doi.org/10.1002/pits.21980.

Department for Education (2011) Behaviour and discipline in schools: A guide for headteachers and school staff. Available from: https://assets.publishing.service.gov.uk/government/uploads/system/uploads/attachment_data/file/353921/Behaviour_and_Discipline_in_Schools_-_A_guide_for_headteachers_and_school_staff.pdf.

Department for Education (2014) Mental health and behaviour in schools (updated regularly). Available from: https://www.gov.uk/government/publications/mental-health-and-behaviour-in-schools-2.

Department for Education (2016) Behaviour and discipline in schools: A guide for headteachers and school leaders. Available from: https://www.gov.uk/government/publications/behaviour-and-discipline-in-schools.

Department for Education and Skills (2003) Every Child Matters: Statutory guidance. UK Government. Available from: https://www.gov.uk/government/publications/every-child-matters-statutory-guidance.

Department for Education and Skills (2005) Learning behaviour: The report of the Practitioners' Group on School Behaviour and Discipline. Available from: https://www.education-uk.org/documents/pdfs/2005-steer-report-learning-behaviour.pdf.

Education Endowment Foundation (2018) Metacognition and self-regulation. Available from: https://educationendowmentfoundation.org.uk/education-evidence/guidance-reports/metacognition.

Education Endowment Foundation (2019) Improving behaviour in schools. Available from: https://educationendowmentfoundation.org.uk/public/files/Publications/Behaviour/EEF_Improving_behaviour_in_schools_Report.pdf.

Ellis, S., & Tod, J. (2014) *Behaviour for Learning: Promoting Positive Relationships in the Classroom*. Abingdon: Routledge.

Fullan, M. (2007) *The New Meaning of Educational Change*. 4th ed. New York, NY: Teachers College Press.

Gruenert, S., & Whitaker, T. (2015) *School Culture Rewired: How to Define, Assess, and Transform It*. Alexandria, VA: ASCD.

ImpactED (2024) Understanding attendance. Available from: https://www.evaluation.impactedgroup.uk/research-and-resources/understanding-attendance.

Ofsted (2014) Below the radar: Low-level disruption in the country's classrooms. Available from: https://assets.publishing.service.gov.uk/media/5a7dcf3b40f0b65d8b4e3a1c/Below_20the_20radar_20-_20low-level_20disruption_20in_20the_20country_E2_80_99s_20classrooms.pdf.

Riley, A., Jones, B., & Smith, C. (2020) The impact of school attendance on academic achievement: A longitudinal study. *Journal of Educational Research*, 45(3), 220–35.

Scottish Government (2017) Primary-secondary transitions: A systematic literature review. Available from: https://www.gov.scot/publications/primary-secondary-transitions-systematic-literature-review-research-findings/pages/1/.

Taylor, C. (2011) Getting the simple things right: Behaviour checklists for headteachers. Department for Education. Available from: https://www.gov.uk/government/news/simple-behaviour-checklist-to-help-teachers-maintain-discipline-in-school.

Webster-Stratton, C., & Reid, M. J. (2010) Adapting the incredible years, an evidence-based parenting programme, for families involved in the child welfare system. *Journal of Children's Services*, 5(1), 25–42.

Wiliam, D. (2011) *Embedded Formative Assessment*. Indiana: Solution Tree Press.

Wiliam, D. (2017) *Embedded Formative Assessment*. 2nd ed. Bloomington, IN: Solution Tree Press, 134.

Woodhouse, J., & Lalic, M. (2024) The impact of smartphones and social media on children. House of Commons Library 13 May. https://commonslibrary.parliament.uk/research-briefings/cdp-2024-0103/.

9

Pastoral Matters and Emotional Wellbeing

Charlotte Bagnall

Overview of chapter

This chapter will focus on the importance of supporting children's emotional wellbeing during educational transitions (which can be defined as the process of changing schools, e.g. moving from one school system [such as primary school] to another [secondary school]). A particular focus will be placed on the transitions from primary school to secondary school, which children make internationally between the ages of ten and fourteen.

To do this, the chapter will discuss the importance of sensitive pastoral care provision, with a dedicated emotional-centred transition curriculum, leading up to and over educational transitions. This support should be informed by theory, research (especially studies which examine key stakeholders' perspectives and experiences during educational transitions), educational policy and practice, which will be discussed within this chapter.

The chapter will end with a critical discussion of existing primary–secondary school transition intervention research within the field and a real-world case study of the design, implementation and evaluation of the *Talking about School Transition 5–7* curriculum (Bagnall & Stevenson, 2024). This universal curriculum was developed to overcome practical and empirical limitations within the field to improve children's emotional wellbeing over primary-secondary school transitions.

Current context of educational transitions

Internationally, staged educational transitions generally occur between the ages of ten and fifteen years. In other words, normative educational transitions are age-graded, with children moving between two tiers (e.g. where children make one educational transition, such as the transition from primary school to secondary school in England and Australia at age eleven or twelve) or three tiers (e.g. where children make two different educational transitions, such as the transition from elementary to middle school at age eleven and then to high school at age fourteen in the United States) of schooling at a specific age and stage in development.

In addition to age-graded transitions which are predetermined by the local authority school system and are typically negotiated for all children at the same time, it is worth noting that some children negotiate non-normative educational transitions. This may include placement transfers (where children transition between different types of school placement, e.g. from mainstream school to special school) and school mobility transfers (e.g. non-normative transitions, which can occur at any time within the school trajectory, for example due to the relocation of the family).

Transition age/timing and impact of place

To date, there is no consensus internationally or even within individual countries on the most appropriate age for children to make educational transitions, despite commissioned research starting in the 1920s in England. For example, research (including my own) has suggested that generally children who are older when they transition schools show more positive social, academic and emotional adjustment. The reason for this is that the older children are when they transition schools, the more likely they have been exposed to previous life transitions, such as moving to a new house, and as a result can adapt to similar challenges inherent in school transition, such as school environment adaptations (e.g. moving between lessons for different subjects), more easily.

Moreover, when transition timing is delayed, such as the transition from middle school to high school in the United States at age fourteen, children have had longer to gain developmental skills, such as emotional intelligence, necessary to successfully navigate challenges inherent in school transitions more easily, whether that is disagreements with peers, environmental discontinuities or academic changes. For example, middle schools (that teach children from age nine to age fourteen in England, and eleven to fourteen in the United States) have advantages over secondary schools, by providing children with consistency, in terms of being taught by the same teacher and in the same school environment, with the same pastoral support, which is often more sensitive and focused on this developmental age. This can be helpful for children during early puberty, as shown in my own case study research in the United States (Bagnall et al., 2021b), and reduce feelings of instability associated with puberty, which is believed to impact children's cognitive and social processing.

Similar research has been shown in Australia, which compared two different types of school transitions: a 'traditional' model where students transition from a K-6 school at age twelve to a 7–10 high school and secondly a P-10 school model, to find that girls were significantly more anxious in Year 7 at high school compared to their K-10 counterparts (Nguyen et al., 2024). However, after eight months of Year 7, students in the traditional model were shown to fare better academically, socially in terms of student-student relations and in their feelings of school identification, which demonstrates the need to examine outcomes over time, given the instability of this period.

In sum, these two ideas are in conflict, as while transition appears to be better the older children are, the transition, when it happens, is a bigger 'leap'. This might be more noticeable in the United States because children have navigated different systems, with those within the two-tier K-8 system appearing to other children and adults as not quite as prepared for high school transition as children within three-tier junior high or middle school systems. This may be because within three-tier school systems, where children attend three different schools, children may find transitioning to their third school easier, reflecting the insight and skills gained from their first transition. However, the first transition is likely to be harder as they will make it at a much younger age, which is especially important when considering educational transitions from infant school to junior school in the UK, which children make at the early age of seven years. Therefore, it is unclear which school system is best for children and the optimal age for school transition, and further research is needed in this area.

Key takeaways:

- School transition is easier when it matches children's disposition and needs, e.g. when children are older, been exposed to prior transition and are well supported.
- When educational transitions are made earlier in development, greater hands-on, sensitive emotional support is needed, with a balance between exposure and consistency.
- Presenting the transition as a progression as opposed to a loss, where focus is on skill-development, can be especially important for children navigating three-tier educational transition systems.

The need to support children's emotional wellbeing

Nonetheless, what *is* known is the need to support children's emotional wellbeing, through sensitive pastoral support, during educational transitions. Educational transitions, such as primary–secondary school transitions, are critical developmental periods, which are believed to have positive and negative impacts on children's emotional wellbeing and mental health. During this time, children negotiate multiple, simultaneous changes, which can be emotionally demanding. In addition to this, educational transitions also often occur at a time when children are experiencing hormonal changes associated with puberty, and in England school-based pressures, such as academic national Standard Assessment Tests. These added stressors can further impact children's cognitive and social processing and perpetuate feelings of instability and anxiety accompanying the change of school in this stage of development.

Unsurprisingly, negotiating multiple changes, during a critical period in development, can heavily draw on children's ability to cope and compromise their emotional wellbeing in the short and long term. In the short term, leading up to and during initial primary–secondary school transition, many children report feeling nervous, anxious and unsettled. My research has suggested that this is often due to a mismatch between the anxiety children experience during primary–secondary transitions and the emotional skills they can draw on to cope, with many children discussing the importance, but also difficulty, in managing their emotions over primary–secondary school transitions (Bagnall, 2020). Furthermore, during primary–secondary school transitions, many children report feeling that they had underestimated the importance of the socio-emotional aspects of the transitions when in primary school, and as a result feel insufficiently prepared for transfer challenges, as shown in my intervention research (Bagnall et al., 2021a).

If prolonged, and support is not provided, children who experience poor emotional wellbeing following primary–secondary school transitions are more at risk of developing poor mental health, in addition to poor academic attainment and social adjustment (Symonds et al., 2023). These outcomes can potentially contribute to poor life chances and exacerbate existing social inequalities. Thus, supporting children's emotional wellbeing, during critical turning points, such as educational transitions, is paramount. This is recognized by key stakeholders, including parents and children, as shown in my own qualitative research (Bagnall et al., 2019), where both transfer parents and children discussed the importance and need for emotional-centred discussions leading up to the transition within primary schools. This was quantified in McGee and colleagues' (2003) survey research, which found 45 per cent of parents to report their child needing help talking about their feelings in preparation for primary–secondary school transitions.

> ### Key takeaways:
>
> - Knowledge of how best to support children's emotional wellbeing over primary–secondary school transitions has the potential to improve mental health and educational trajectories across the life course
> - To do this, primary–secondary school transition provision needs to be gradual and sensitive, with a clear balance between exposure and consistency. This can help to manage children's expectations, so that they feel prepared but not overwhelmed by their next chapter.

Educational policy

Within educational policy, educational transitions became a mandatory area examined in UK Office for Standards in Education, Children's Services and Skills (OFSTED) inspections in 2007. This policy was introduced to prevent variability in transition provision. However, over the past decade, government reports are still reporting primary–secondary school transitions as a period 'not handled well' (Ofsted, 2015, March, p. 65). The quality of transition between Key Stage 2 and Key Stage 3 is reported to be still 'much too variable' (Ofsted, 2015, September, p. 21) and arrangements for transfer as a result are 'weak in over a quarter of the schools visited' (Ofsted, 2014, p. 21). As a result, it has been acknowledged that there needs to be 'a greater focus on transition periods in children and young people's lives' as current transition interventions 'do not give enough importance to improving resilience and wellbeing and how schools and colleges might be supported in this role' (DfE, 2018, p. 13).

The importance of supporting children's emotional wellbeing over primary–secondary school transitions has been further intensified by the international outbreak of Covid-19, which heightened the negative impact of primary–secondary school transitions on children's emotional wellbeing (Bagnall et al., 2022), and there is evidence to suggest that schools are still recovering (Garner & Bagnall, 2024). Thus, there is need to intervene, taking an early preventative approach by focusing on supporting children's short- and long-term emotional wellbeing. This is especially given the stretched time and financial resources schools face to address preventative mental health concerns, but also recognizes longitudinal research findings which have shown emotional wellbeing to predict changes in mental health over time within adolescent populations (Petersen et al., 2022).

Key takeaways:

- A systemic approach to primary–secondary school transition provision is needed, with emotional wellbeing central to this.
- Education policymakers should encourage implementation of a sensitive primary–secondary school transition curriculum. The *Talking about School Transition 5–7* intervention is a good example of this (and is discussed below), and support for this as a 'promising school-based intervention' has been referenced in recent NICE (07/22) and Health Policy Scotland guidelines (01/20), and has been supported by the Minister for Children, Families and Wellbeing (01/24).
- The Department for Education and Local Authorities should work with educators to further develop and implement this transition curriculum more widely, especially within the post Covid-19 recovery context.

Intervention research and *Talking about School Transitions 5–7* case study

Recognizing that primary–secondary school transitions are a critical period for children that pose heightened risk for the development of poor emotional wellbeing, educational transitions provide a key entrance point for intervention work. For example, in my own research, we have found that most children report feelings of stress and anxiety about moving to secondary school from as early as Year 5 (second to last year in primary school in England) in primary school (Bagnall et al., 2024), which can continue two years into secondary school (Jindal-Snape & Cantali, 2019). Thus, there is need to take a preventative approach over primary–secondary school transitions by explicitly focusing on supporting children's emotional wellbeing, taking a gradual, progressive approach, beginning in Year 5 and continuing into Year 7, which is in line with longitudinal developmental cascade studies. However, at face value there appears to be many programmes developed to improve children's experiences of primary–secondary school transitions. However, from a review of existing literature (Beatson et al., 2023), primary–secondary school transitions research is limited by:

(1) not holistically evaluating the impact on children (e.g. research has looked at 'transition specific concepts' such as social and academic adjustment with a lack of focus on children's emotional wellbeing);
(2) intervention design (e.g. there is a lack of early-intervention support, with no programmes beginning in Year 5); and
(3) weaker evaluation (e.g. there is no intervention evaluations which have measured outcomes at the individual level (e.g. following the same group of children) across three school years [beginning in Year 5]), using both quantitative and qualitative approaches, which is needed to obtain the lived experiences of the children and teachers participating in these programmes.

The *Talking about School Transition 5–7 (TaST 5–7)* intervention, which is a seventeen-week universal, skills-based transition curriculum, beginning in Year 5 and continuing into Year 7, aims to overcome this gap by developing children's awareness and ability to cope with the multiple changes they will

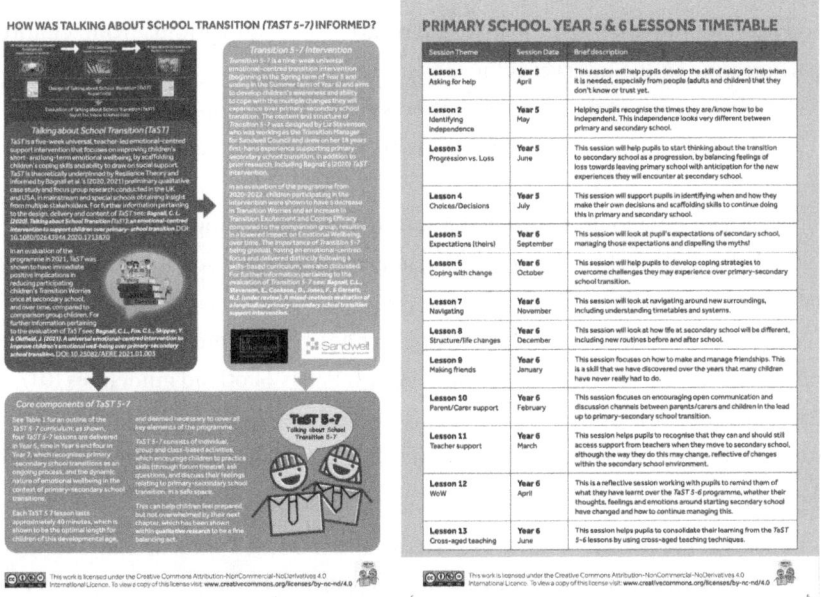

Figure 9.1 The design of Talking about School Transitions 5–7 (TaST 5–7).

experience over primary–secondary school transition. *TaST 5–7* is informed by theory (*Multiple and Multi-dimensional Transitions* Theory; Jindal-Snape, 2023) and prior empirical research, including the design and evaluation of my *Talking about School Transition (TaST)* intervention, in addition to experienced practitioner Liz Stevenson's *Transition 5–7* intervention, which are outlined below, and in Figure 9.1.

Talking about School Transition (TaST) is a five-week emotional-centred intervention that focuses on supporting children's emotional wellbeing over primary–secondary school transitions, by scaffolding children's coping skills and ability to draw on social support from parents/guardians, teachers and classmates. *TaST* is theoretically underpinned by Resilience Theory, in addition to qualitative case study and focus group research I conducted in the UK (Bagnall et al., 2019) and the United States (Bagnall et al., 2021b), in mainstream and special schools (Bagnall et al., 2021c).

Outcome evaluation: *TaST* was shown to have immediate positive implications in reducing participating children's transition worries once at secondary school, and over time, compared to comparison group children.

Process evaluation: Children not only expressed how *TaST* focussed on variables associated with coping, such as their emotions, appraisals and coping efficacy, but also discussed how these skills would likely help them when they transitioned to secondary school, managing children's expectations and developing their confidence. Here are some quotations from children participating in the intervention:

'it filled me with confidence about how to deal with things';

'it showed you how to cope in different situations, and helped me to be more prepared';

'we learnt how to deal with being scared and to think more positively';

'it helped me calm down about going to secondary school because I was nervous to start with, so it was very useful'.

Support for *TaST* as a 'promising school-based intervention' has been referenced in recent NICE (07/22) and Health Policy Scotland guidelines (01/22) following my research. This intervention has now been implemented across multiple local authorities in the UK and shown to have international impact in Melbourne in Australia:

> *from our perspective none of this would have happened without TaST, which has transformed Victoria's approach to supporting primary-secondary school transition, and even the Department of Education in Victoria are now becoming a lot more aware of this need. TaST reduced children's anxiety, increased their*

awareness about transition and ultimately gave them the language to feel more comfortable.

(Mental Health Practitioner)

Transition 5–7 is a nine-week universal, class-based, transition intervention, delivered from the Spring term of Year 5 to the Summer term of Year 6. *Transition 5–7* aims to develop children's awareness and ability to cope with the multiple changes children experience over primary–secondary school transitions, through a forum theatre skills-based curriculum. The content and structure of *Transition 5–7* was informed and designed by Liz Stevenson's eighteen years' first-hand experience supporting primary–secondary school transition.

Outcome evaluation: The outcome evaluation found that children participating in the intervention showed a decrease in transition worries and an increase in transition excitement and coping efficacy compared to the comparison group from Year 5 to Year 6, resulting in a lowered impact on emotional wellbeing in Year 7.

Process evaluation: The importance of *Transition 5–7* being gradual, having an emotional-centred focus and being delivered distinctly following a skills-based curriculum was discussed in the process evaluation focus groups and interviews. Here are some quotations from teachers participating in the intervention:

'It was really good starting earlier, yeah. They were able to take it in more as well, than last minute lessons, you know, after SATS at the end of Year 6, they're more well prepared if they hear it beforehand.' (Teacher 2)

'These are mindset changes for the children, these are skill changes that need to come to form habits which take time.' (Teacher 1)

'what I thought was most helpful was giving us realistic situations that will happen in secondary school'. (Focus group 3)

'the lessons formed a safe place where you can ask questions'. (Focus group 2)

'So, at first, I felt quite anxious about what was going to happen and then I felt fine because at least I know what's going to happen and everyone's probably going to be in the same boat as me.' (Focus group 3)

Talking about School Transitions 5–7

Together, the design, implementation and evaluations of *TaST* and *Transition 5–7* informed the development of the *TaST 5–7* curriculum. The curriculum includes four lessons which are delivered in Year 5, nine lessons delivered in Year 6, and four lessons delivered in Year 7. Each *TaST 5–7* lesson lasts approximately forty minutes, which is shown to be the optimal length for children of this developmental age, and deemed necessary to cover all key elements of the programme. *TaST 5–7* consists of individual, group and class-based drama activities, which aim to improve children's spoken and written emotional expression in preparation for the transition to secondary school. Finally, recognizing primary–secondary school transitions as an ongoing process, and the dynamic nature of emotional wellbeing in the context of primary–secondary school transitions, *TaST 5–7* starts in May in Year 5, and continues into Year 7, with the last lesson taking place in December in Year 7.

The principle aim of the curriculum is to support the development of more positive feelings towards primary–secondary school transitions over Year 5 and 6 in primary school, and into the first two terms of Year 7 in secondary school, leading to greater emotional wellbeing. *TaST 5–7* aims to do this by increasing children's belief in their ability to cope with the multiple changes they will experience over primary–secondary school transition, by developing children's transition knowledge and positive coping strategies (specifically emotional self-efficacy). These aims are in line with previous research which has shown children's adjustment over primary–secondary school transitions to be shaped by individual-level factors, such as coping efficacy and emotional intelligence, external factors such as school size, culture and ethos (and children's awareness of these factors beforehand), and social factors such as positive, supportive relationships with parents/carers, teachers and peers (Bagnall & Jindal-Snape, 2023). *TaST 5–7* aims to support the development of individual-level factors, through developing children's knowledge and awareness of the multiple changes they will negotiate over primary–secondary school transitions, and skills in being able to manage discontinuity, through providing children with opportunities to 'test-out' learnt transitions strategies, through forum theatre, alongside their classmates.

My research team are currently trialling the *TaST 5–7* skills-based curriculum, alongside the design and validation of our *#P-S WELLS* scale development and validation research study (discussed below), which aims to identify: *(a)* which aspects of moving to secondary school children are experiencing emotional difficulties with, and *when, (b) who* might be particularly vulnerable and *(c) what* support could be useful, on a universal, whole-class basis, but also on a targeted 1:1 or group basis. From an intervention science perspective, *#P-S WELLS* will provide a tool for researchers to (a) evaluate the efficacy of pre-existing emotional wellbeing and mental health support interventions in the context of primary–secondary school transitions; (b) refine the content and delivery of pre-existing programmes, by strengthening the methodological and conceptual foundations that underpin primary–secondary school transitions and mental health research; and (c) provide the means for sensitive identification of 'at risk' children to participate in targeted interventions. Findings will be shared in 2026. You can find further information about the progress of this research project here: https://www.p-s-wells.org.

> ### Key takeaways:
>
> - Contiguous primary–secondary school transitions provision running from Year 5 until the end of Year 7 is best practice, with focus on children's emotional wellbeing at the forefront.
> - This provision should take a gradual and 'non-threatening' progressive approach, by initially focussing on the development of skills, such as asking for help and making decisions, that will be useful over primary–secondary school transitions, before directly discussing primary–secondary school transitions.
> - Transition lessons should follow a skills-based curriculum, and focus on developing children's awareness, knowledge and ability to cope with the multiple changes experienced over primary–secondary school transitions, by encouraging children to test out strategies, ask questions and discuss their feelings in a safe space.

Implications for teaching and leadership staff

To summarize, educational transitions, such as primary–secondary school transitions, are critical developmental periods, and an important turning point in establishing the foundations for nurturing long-term positive emotional well-being and mental health. Therefore, primary–secondary school transitions are a key entrance point for early-intervention emotional wellbeing support. To varying degrees, schools adopt a range of interventions to prepare and support children during this time, which can be categorized into three broad strategies: school administration (e.g. sharing of pupil information), teaching and learning (e.g. curriculum continuity and pedagogy) and socio-emotional support (e.g. pastoral support, lessons focussed on developing social and emotional skills, such as *TaST 5–7*). This chapter has focused on the latter, and below I have outlined some implications for teaching and leadership staff:

- **Emotional-centred, skills-based curriculum**

Education policymakers should encourage implementation of a sensitive primary–secondary school transition curriculum, which takes an early-intervention approach, running from Year 5 in primary school until at least the end of the second term in Year 7 in secondary school. This curriculum should be cohesive across both primary school and secondary school and include targeted support for children's emotional wellbeing. *TaST 5–7* is a good example of this, and The Department for Education and Local Authorities should work with educators to further develop and implement this transition curriculum more widely, especially acknowledging that support across schools within local authorities can be variable (Garner & Bagnall, 2024).

This curriculum should be 'skills-based', with lessons focussing on developing children's awareness, knowledge and ability to cope with the multiple changes experienced over primary–secondary school transitions. This can be done by providing opportunity for children to practice skills that will be useful over primary–secondary school transitions, such as remembering equipment to bring in for a specific lesson; asking questions, such as what to do if they were to get lost; and discussing their feelings about transitioning to secondary school in a safe space, following a balanced discourse, with focus on both worries and excitement. This can help children feel prepared, but not overwhelmed, by their next chapter, which has been shown within my qualitative research to be a fine balancing act, to ensure children do not feel falsely prepared (Bagnall et al., 2019).

In sum, and as discussed above, the aim of primary–secondary school transitions curriculums is to make it clear that transition challenges cannot be removed. Instead, importance should be placed on helping children to develop new skills and 'habits' to help them adjust to the new secondary school setting and help children recognize, understand and manage their emotions during this time.

- **Transition timing and continued support into Year 7**

As discussed above, transition provision is best placed when children have sufficient time to gradually prepare for their next chapter. As shown through the process and outcome evaluation findings of the *Transition 5–7* intervention, beginning two years prior to secondary school in Year 5 in primary school is especially important in nurturing children's perceptions of their ability to cope leading up to primary–secondary school transitions.

Practitioners delivering the *Transition 5–7* intervention discussed the importance of sessions being spread evenly across Year 5 and 6 in primary school to help facilitate a gradual pace of transitions provision. This provided greater opportunities for children to be exposed to school transition knowledge and practice transition skills, within a safe space, prior to secondary school. Recognizing this, reserving class time (e.g. during PSHE lessons in England) during Year 5 and 6 for primary–secondary school transition provision, is paramount, as is an element of flexibility for class teachers to select the week, day and time for each session. This not only demonstrates the complexity of implementing emotional-centred transition support during this time but also has implications for leadership staff, in providing designating time and flexibility within the curriculum for pastoral support focussed on primary–secondary school transitions.

Primary–secondary school transition provision needs to follow a systemic approach and be continued into Year 7, through bridging programmes. Supporting children's emotional wellbeing should be central to this, by following a cohesive transition curriculum, such as *TaST 5–7*, which follows a shared language. Supporting the development of children's emotional literacy in the lead up to primary–secondary school transitions and then continuing this support into secondary school can help children recognize, understand and manage their changing emotions, and be especially protective for more vulnerable children, such as children with special educational needs (SEND) or who have experienced Adverse Childhood Experiences (ACEs).

- **Levels of intervention and *P-S WELLS***

It is also worth noting that some children, such as those with SEND, who experienced ACEs, in receipt of Pupil Premium Funding (PP) and have been or are at risk of being excluded and/or suspended, may need further targeted support over primary–secondary school transitions, beyond universal provision (e.g. support delivered to all children within a class, such as the *TaST 5–7* curriculum). This support may include elements of proportionate universalism (e.g. for children identified as requiring additional support, the intensity of the intervention might increase; for example, they might receive longer intervention lessons, or more frequent follow-on support). Targeted small transition support groups or pyramid clubs, providing more focused and sensitive support, may also be useful. The aim of targeted approaches is to help prevent the widening of disadvantage and vulnerability.

Furthermore, improving collaboration and communication channels across systems (e.g. primary school and secondary school) and stakeholders (e.g. parents/carers and educators) may also be helpful for more at risk children, ensuring all voices are heard, including the child's. This could be facilitated at the local authority level and would ensure that our most vulnerable children and their parents/guardians receive continuity in standards and support adjusted to meet their individual needs. It would also support their short- and long-term emotional wellbeing and help children feel safe and a sense of control of their transition, which is shown to be paramount during this time, especially for children with additional social, emotional and mental health needs (Bagnall et al., 2021c).

To do this, early detection of children who may be at risk of poor primary–secondary school transition experiences and providing them with additional support tailored to their individual needs is paramount. As a first step in doing, my team and I at the University of Manchester and University of Dundee are developing a scale to measure children's emotional wellbeing in the context of primary–secondary school transitions. This novel instrument is called the *Primary-Secondary School Transitions Emotional Wellbeing Scale (#P-S WELLS)* and will have significant empirical and practical utility, by enabling researchers and practitioners to identify:

a. **Which** aspects of primary–secondary school transitions children are excited about, as well as concerned about
b. **Who** might be particularly vulnerable during primary–secondary school transitions
c. **What** universal and targeted support could be useful

#P-S WELLS will add distinct value at a community level by developing a tool and manual to build capacity for educational practitioners to obtain immediate insight into the universal support their class needs and identification of specific children who need additional support. Education policymakers and local authorities should engage with the development and rollout of this instrument and advocate embedding this into a transition curriculum.

At each phase of the *#P-S WELLS* research study, we are working in close consultation with experts by experience (e.g. children, educational practitioners, policy makers) and experts by knowledge (e.g. researchers with empirical, theoretical, methodological and policy expertise), to design, pilot and validate our scale. If you, or your school, are interested in assisting at any phase of our project, please get in touch via our project email address: PS-wells@manchester.ac.uk

Further reading

Bagnall, C.L., Jindal-Snape, D., Panayiotou, M., & Qualter, P. (2024). Design and validation of the Primary-Secondary School Transitions Emotional Wellbeing Scale (P-S WELLS); the first instrument to assess children's emotional wellbeing in the context of primary-secondary school transitions. *International Journal of Educational and Life Transitions*, 3(1), 4. doi: 10.5334/ijelt.79.

For further information pertaining to the progress of the design and validation of the *Primary-Secondary School Transitions Emotional Wellbeing Scale (P-S WELLS)*, see our project website: https://www.p-s-wells.org.

References

Bagnall, C.L., Skipper, Y., & Fox, C.L. (2019) 'You're in this world now': Students', teachers', and parents' experiences of school transition and how they feel it can be improved. *British Journal of Educational Psychology*, 90, 206–26. doi: 10.1111/bjep.12273.

Bagnall, C.L. (2020) Talking about School Transition (TaST): An emotional-centred intervention to support children over primary-secondary school transition. *Pastoral Care in Education*, 38(2), 116–37. doi: 10.1080/02643944.2020.1713870.

Bagnall, C.L., Fox, C.L., Skipper, Y., & Oldfield, J. (2021a) Evaluating a universal emotional-centred intervention to improve children's emotional well-being over primary-secondary school transition. *Advances in Educational Research and Evaluation*, 2, 113–26. doi: 10.25082/AERE.2021.01.003.

Bagnall, C.L., Fox, C.L., & Skipper, Y. (2021b) When is the 'optimal' time for school transition? An insight into provision in the US. *Pastoral Care in Education*, 39(4), 348–76. doi: 10.1080/02643944.2020.1855669.

Bagnall, C.L., Fox, C.L., & Skipper, Y. (2021c) What emotional-centred challenges do special schools face over primary-secondary school transition? *Journal of Research in Special Educational Needs*, 21, 156–67. doi: 10.1111/1471-3802.12507.

Bagnall, C.L., Skipper, Y., & Fox, C.L. (2022) Understanding children's, parents'/guardians', and teachers' experiences of primary-secondary school transition in the context of the Covid-19 lockdown: How can this inform transition provision now and in the future? *British Journal of Educational Psychology*, 92, 1011–33. doi: 10.1111/bjep.12485.

Bagnall, C.L., & Jindal-Snape, D. (2023) Child self-report measures of primary-secondary transition experiences and emotional wellbeing: An international systematic literature review. *International Journal of Educational and Life Transitions*, 2(1), 4, 1–31. doi: 10.5334/ijelt.35.

Bagnall, C.L., Cookson, D., Stevenson, E., Jones, F., & Garnett, N.J. (2024a) Evaluation of a longitudinal transition support intervention to improve children's emotional well-being and adjustment over primary-secondary school transition. *Frontiers Educational Psychology*, 15, 1–17. doi: 10.3389/fpsyg.2024.1252851.

Bagnall, C.L., Jindal-Snape, D., Panayiotou, M., & Qualter, P. (2024b) Design and validation of the Primary-Secondary School Transitions Emotional Wellbeing Scale (P-S WELLS); the first instrument to assess children's emotional wellbeing in the context of primary-secondary school transitions. *International Journal of Educational and Life Transitions*, 3(1), 4. doi: 10.5334/ijelt.79.

Bagnall, C.L., & Stevenson, E. (2024) Talking about School Transitions 5–7 *(TaST 5–7)*. Available from: *https://www.p-s-wells.org/tast-5-7*.

Beatson, R., Quach, J., Canterford, L., Farrow, P., Bagnall, C., Hockey, P., ... & Mundy, L. (2023) Improving primary to secondary school transitions: A systematic review of school-based interventions to prepare and support student social-emotional and educational outcomes. *Educational Research Review*, 40, 100553. https://doi.org/10.1016/j.edurev.2023.100553.

Department of Health and Social Care and Department for Education (2018) *Transforming Children and Young People's Mental Health Provision: A Green Paper*. London. Available from: https://assets.publishing.service.gov.uk/government/uploads/system/uploads/attachment_data/file/664855/Transforming_children_and_young_people_s_mental_health_provision.pdf.

Garner, E., & Bagnall, C.L. (2024) Transition from primary to secondary school in greater Manchester: A qualitative exploration of the perspectives of year 6 children who receive pupil premium funding. *British Educational Research Journal*, 50, 2663–83. https://doi.org/10.1002/berj.4045.

Jindal-Snape, D., & Cantali, D. (2019) A four-stage longitudinal study exploring pupils' experiences, preparation and support systems during primary–secondary school transitions. *British Educational Research Journal*, 45(6), 1255–78. doi: https://doi.org/10.1002/berj.3561.

McGee, C., Ward, R., Gibbons, J., & Harlow, A. (2003) Transition to secondary school: A literature review. A Report to the Ministry of Education. Available from www.minedu.govt.nzb.

Nguyen, K., & Reynolds, K.J. (2024) School structure and school outcomes: Comparing primary to high school transitions in traditional and P-10 schools in the ACT. Science at the Australian National University.

Ofsted (2014) *Ofsted Annual Report 2013/14*. London.

Ofsted (2015) The most able students: An update on progress since June 2013. March. Available from: www.gov.uk/government/publications/the-mostable-students-an-update-on-progress-sincejune-2013.

Ofsted (2015) Key stage 3: The wasted years? September. Available from: www.gov.uk/government/publications/key-stage-3-the-wasted-years.

Petersen, K.J., Humphrey, N., & Qualter, P. (2022) Dual-factor mental health from childhood to early adolescence and associated factors: A latent transition analysis. *Journal of Youth and Adolescence, 51*(6), 1118–33. https://doi.org/10.1007/s10964-021-01550-9.

Symonds, J. E., Jindal-Snape, D., Bagnall, C., Hannah, E. F., & Barlow, W. (2023) School transitions in human and adolescent development. In: *Reference Module in Neuroscience and Biobehavioral Psychology* (pp. 306–13). Elsevier.

10

The Impact of Disadvantage on Educational Transitions

Elizabeth Gregory

Overview of chapter

This chapter examines the impact that disadvantage can have on transitions across the education life course, with a particular focus on poverty and the English schooling system. Without appropriate support, the potential challenges of educational transitions discussed elsewhere in this book can be greatly heightened for children from low-income backgrounds. The case study highlighted in this chapter reports on the work of Local Matters, a research project operating across the north of England that tackles disadvantage in schools by empowering teachers to understand what poverty looks like in their local area. Thus, whilst the chapter examines the universal challenges faced by disadvantaged students during the transition process, we also consider the more nuanced aspects of how place may affect children's experiences of transition.

Current policy contexts in England: The impact of austerity on education

At the time of writing, the UK – along with many countries across the world – is in the midst of a cost-of-living crisis, with the price of essential goods and services rising sharply (ONS, 2024). This has prompted some alarming statistics around growing levels of poverty across the UK, with 4.2 million under-16s living in poverty, representing 29 per cent of all UK children (Devine, 2023). As this means that, statistically, ten children in every class of thirty are living in poverty, teachers and school leaders need to be mindful of how best to support their more vulnerable pupils, particularly during periods of transition.

Unfortunately, whilst the current economic situation has prompted some long-overdue discussion of the impact of poverty, all too often political and popular discourses are based around a deficit model. This places a focus on the perceived failings of individuals and their choices rather than addressing the structural inequalities that have resulted in such unequal distribution of material advantages. As we shall see later in the chapter, this culture of blaming the individual can affect the way that children from lower-income backgrounds are perceived and impact upon their experiences of transitioning to a new school.

Another prevalent discourse around educational opportunities uses the language of meritocracy and social mobility to emphasize the responsibility of the individual child to aim high and achieve despite these inequalities. This frequently positions schools – and education in general – as potential engines of social change, offering the chance of success to any child who puts the effort in. Many of us will remember David Cameron's 2012 Conservative party conference speech where he declared that a 'toxic culture of low expectations – that lack of ambition for every child – which has held this country back' (Cameron, 2012), and Theresa May's call for Britain to be the 'world's great meritocracy – a country where everyone has a fair chance to go as far as their talent and their hard work will allow' (May, 2016).

Some additional finance is available for schools in England to support individual pupils from lower-income backgrounds. This includes the Pupil Premium payment made directly to schools for each looked-after child and each child receiving or previously in receipt of Free School Meals (FSM) (Department for Education, 2024a), which aims to improve educational outcomes for disadvantaged pupils in state-funded schools. However, as this chapter will explore, individualized support can only go so far in addressing the more systemic inequalities students can face during transitional periods. Indeed, eligibility for FSM as an indicator of family income is much contested for a number of reasons, including feelings of shame or language barriers preventing families applying for the support to which they are entitled. It is worth noting that schools are reliant on families applying for FSM; if the family don't claim, the school cannot receive.

At this point, it is pertinent to include a note on the term 'disadvantage', which can itself viewed as problematic by suggesting a lack or deficit, and can be perceived as negatively dividing individuals into the 'haves' and the 'have-nots'. Similarly, it can be claimed that one single term is inadequate in capturing the huge range of circumstances that can affect how individuals and families live their lives. Thus, the chapter discusses disadvantage as a situation in which some families have a lower level of household and/or disposable income that can lead to lifestyle restrictions, whilst also recognizing that such terminology can oversimplify complex issues around poverty.

> ## Key takeaways:
>
> - At time of writing, more children and families are living in poverty.
> - Discourses around individual blame and deficit are common when discussing poverty.
> - Ideas around meritocracy and social mobility can disguise the structural inequalities in society.

Managing academic and curriculum changes

Whose capital is valued in the curriculum?

One of the exciting opportunities offered by transition is the chance to study new topics and explore new curricula in greater depth. This is particularly true of the move to secondary school, where a whole range of new subjects is studied, and existing knowledge of subjects studied at primary school is deepened. These subjects and their content are, in England, determined by the National Curriculum, which prescribes what students must learn in order to be well prepared for the standardized tests that are taken at the end of each stage of schooling.

However, pupils from lower-income backgrounds may, at times, struggle to see themselves represented in the material taught in class. Sometimes this may be outside the control of schools and their teaching staff; a recent (2022) GCSE English Language paper, for example, attracted much criticism for asking pupils to argue whether or not holidays needed to be expensive, overseas trips or whether something closer to home could be just as relaxing – showing a complete lack of awareness that many pupils might have limited experience of any type of holiday at all.

Similarly, in 2016 the Year 6 SATs reading paper featured a moat in the grounds of a home and the extinction of the dodo—hardly topics that are universally relatable. This example is particularly problematic in terms of transitions, as secondary schools use SATs results to judge pupils' abilities. However, as we shall see in our case study later in the chapter, there are plenty of things that schools can do to make new pupils from all backgrounds feel welcome.

Barriers to accessing a new curriculum

Adapting to academic and curriculum changes poses a much larger challenge when pupils are not able to attend consistently, with school absenteeism due to restricted finances becoming commonplace in recent years. Writing about high levels of pupil absences from school following the lockdowns of 2020 and 2021, Diane Reay points out that poverty presents a number of barriers for children from disadvantaged backgrounds in accessing school on a regular basis and notes that absenteeism is a class issue (Reay, 2024). She also argues that 'teaching to the test' is the predominant approach in working-class schools, leading to anxiety and school avoidance in those pupils who are in most need of support.

So, what form might these barriers to attendance take? Since schools reopened after the lockdowns of 2020 and 2021, pupil absenteeism has been higher than before the pandemic across all socio-economic backgrounds. However, the situation is more acute for those children from less advantaged backgrounds; for example, government figures state that 36.5 per cent of FSM-eligible pupils were persistently absent from school in 2022–3 compared with 15.6 per cent of pupils who were not eligible (Explore Education Statistics, 2024). Additional challenges to overcome can include lack of a clean uniform or other key supplies, lack of money for transport to school or caring duties for other siblings. These problems can be exacerbated by a change of school, which may be further away from home or from other siblings' schools, and where the child's background and/or family situation is not yet known to staff. These matters can be hard for both parents and school staff to broach, as we shall see later in our case study.

Other barriers to accessing a new curriculum and the study habits it entails can become more prevalent during transitions later in the education life course, particularly in terms of needing to combine study with paid work in order to contribute to the family budget or purchase essentials. Students from lower-income backgrounds are far more likely to have to engage with the labour market in this way, leaving them less time to concentrate on their studies and more at risk of dropping out or not passing their course. A survey of 1050 students (Sutton Trust, 2023) indicated that 24 per cent of respondents doubted their ability to complete their degree due to the cost of living crisis, with students from low-income families hit disproportionately highly – only 38 per cent of working-class students were receiving additional support from their parents compared to

48 per cent of respondents from higher-income households. This is just one of many ways in which existing equalities can be exacerbated by external pressures.

The challenges of homework

As we have seen earlier in this book, expectations of independent learning tend to increase significantly each time a student moves to the next stage of their education. This increased workload outside the supportive environment of the classroom is particularly evident for learners moving into secondary school and post-16 education, although as the school lockdowns of 2020 and 2021 demonstrated, an expectation of independent learning has the potential to impact all learners across the life course.

However, the expectation that a learner should adapt to an increase in homework and other forms of independent learning as part of the transition process makes a number of assumptions about the resources that students are able to access outside of school. One challenge that has been well documented recently is lack of access to technology, with shortages of computer equipment and Wi-Fi access at home having a significant impact on pupils' ability to complete independent work outside the classroom. This became particularly apparent during the lockdowns mentioned above, when, according to a survey completed by over 4,000 parents of children aged between four and fifteen, 14 per cent of secondary school children in the least well-off families were using a phone or had no device to access schoolwork, and 58 per cent of primary school students from the least well-off families did not even have access to their own study space (Andrew et al., 2020).

A further assumption often made about students from lower-income backgrounds is that parents are either unwilling or unable to provide support with homework tasks. However, research suggests that a strengthening of the relationship between schools and parents/caregivers could help each engage more successfully with the other to support their children. For example, supporting children with mathematics is a well-documented area of concern for many parents and caregivers but particularly for those from more disadvantaged backgrounds where their own relationship with formal schooling may have been complex (Howker & Black, forthcoming). Their research, centred on a group of parents from a high-poverty community in the North of England, suggests that forming a connection between 'everyday' mathematics and 'school' mathematics could help manage the anxieties around supporting homework such as the one expressed by the following participant:

> Emilia (researcher): next year they'll be bringing more homework back won't they ... like maths and stuff
>
> Bianca (participant): Paddy's [child about to enter year 1] gonna struggle with that ... he's gonna find that hard I'm telling you now ... he can come back here with it but we're not the best ... I'm not the best educated and his dad he's the same as me we didn't do school ... so there's no point them bringing stuff home to do because we haven't got a clue ... Callum [older child in year 5] brings home some stuff and I have to keep saying to them [school] 'look you're gonna have to do it with him because there's no way it's gonna get done otherwise'[...] (Howker & Black, forthcoming).

Further discussion demonstrated that, in fact, Bianca had a fund of practical mathematics knowledge shaped around managing poverty; for example, knowing the cost of ingredients and energy, managing cooking times and temperatures, and encouraging the younger children to play with toy money. Recognizing and valuing such knowledge is one way of fostering confidence amongst families in supporting their children's learning.

Key takeaways:

- Pupils from lower-income backgrounds do not always see themselves represented in the curriculum.
- A number of practical factors such as the cost of getting to school or the need to work alongside studying can introduce further barriers to accessing a new curriculum.
- Students from different backgrounds may well have varying amounts of support at home for completing independent study tasks.

Assessment

Successful transitions often rely upon a satisfactory performance in compulsory, standardized examinations and assessments. Unfortunately, statistics indicate that a low-income background is a strong predictor of lower educational performance and achievement across all stages of the curriculum. For example, transition to post-16 study in England is highly dependent upon achieving a particular number of GCSEs graded A*-C (using the old grading system, now amended to award grades 9-1). A common benchmark used is the achievement of five 'good' GCSEs, but government statistics show that such success is harder to come by for some children than others. Whilst the government continues to refer to a gap in attainment, many institutions have begun instead to refer to an 'awarding gap' in order to recognize that for many pupils, their results are due to societal factors outside their control.

In recent years, government discourses have identified reducing the attainment gap as a priority. However, the reduction has slowed, and in fact the awarding gap is now widening in early years, primary and secondary. Published statistics use eligibility for FSM to indicate which students are from lower-income backgrounds, and whilst this does not always capture family circumstances satisfactorily, as noted above, the figures are still worrying – particularly the trend for this gap to widen as children progress through the schooling system as well as widening over time. In the academic year 2022–3, government data tell us that the disadvantage gap at KS4 when children take their GCSEs, is now at its highest level since 2011, and stands at 3.94 percentage points difference (DfE, 2024b).

For many children and young people, underperforming in tests and exams can make transitions far more challenging. Many schools use ability-based setting to stream students into different classes, both for new pupils and for in-school transitions when students move up to the next school year. As Drummond and Yarker (2013) point out, labelling and grouping pupils by their perceived ability leads to assumptions about children's ability being fixed at a particular level, and thus to deficit models of children and their capacity to learn and achieve. In terms of transitioning to the next stage of education, failing to achieve expected grades can be the difference between being able to follow one's chosen educational pathway or not; gaining high enough GCSE grades to study A-levels at age sixteen, for example, or getting the right grades to go to university.

Key takeaways:

- Despite attempts to lower the attainment gap, children from a low-income background are at increased risk of lower educational performance and achievement across all stages of the curriculum.
- This can mean that children are placed in lower ability-based sets at school, or are not able to progress to their next chosen stage of education.

Managing social and relational changes

Students from low-income backgrounds face the same social challenges as children from more privileged backgrounds, but can face additional hardship through lack of the resources to address or mitigate these new situations.

New relationships with peers

As we have already seen, all learners moving from one stage of education to the next are likely to be at least partially removed from their old friendship group and be placed in a position where new friendships with peers are required. As noted, this can be both a time of opportunity (in leaving old cliques behind) and challenge (the discomfort occasioned by having to build new relationships). For families without access to disposable income, however, the challenges can be exacerbated by a lack of resources to pay for activities where friendships are likely to blossom and/or be cemented; for example, school trips and extracurricular clubs.

Peer relationships can also be threatened by a perception that a student is 'different' or 'deficient' in some way. This can manifest in any number of ways and certainly isn't always linked to poverty! However, peer pressure often includes a certain amount of 'keeping up', which can be challenging for those from lower-income backgrounds. The precise form this takes will vary depending on age and educational setting, but may involve:

- Having a second-hand, poorly fitting or supermarket-branded school uniform;
- Not having the latest clothes to wear on non-uniform days;
- Wearing clothes that are not washed as frequently as those of other students;
- Having free school meals or bringing packed lunches perceived as lacking in some way;
- Walking to school due to lack of transport.

New relationships with school staff

Similarly, educational transitions generally require students to get to know not only new teachers but an entire school or college full of new staff with whom they must interact on a regular basis. In theory, this offers a clean slate to students by giving them the opportunity to start afresh, unrestricted by any negative perceptions that staff may have held about them in their previous school.

However, research suggests that school staff's perceptions of pupils and their abilities can be heavily influenced by their beliefs about a pupil's social class as well as their gender and ethnicity (see, for example, Gillborn, 2006). As we shall see in the case study reported later in this chapter, staff attitudes towards poverty and the children and families who live in disadvantaged neighbourhoods can be surprisingly negative.

Key takeaways:

- Social transitions can be more complex for pupils from lower-income backgrounds, as opportunities to make friends can be less accessible.
- Social integration can also be threatened by material shortages.
- New relationships with school staff can also be harder to navigate due to negative attitudes towards pupils from particular areas or backgrounds.

Impact of place

Inequality of resources

In terms of material resources, schools in areas of deprivation often find themselves at a disadvantage compared to those in wealthier, more privileged areas. Whilst Pupil Premium can provide a lifeline to schools with high numbers of students from lower-income households, many schools are still drastically underfunded and often struggle to attract and retain staff. The Public Accounts Committee has criticized recent government changes to both Pupil Premium funding and the way that schools are funded more generally, claiming that average funding per pupil has fallen by 1.2 per cent in real terms for the most deprived fifth of schools whilst increasing by 2.9 per cent for the least deprived fifth, and that £90 million of Pupil Premium funding has been lost (UK Parliament, 2021). This can make it challenging for schools to invest in appropriate activities to support pupil transitions, or to welcome new students to a well-resourced and appropriately staffed environment where lasting relationships can be built with familiar faces and routines.

Limited study options

The type of school a student attends can also affect their chances of a successful transition due to limits placed on study options (and, as a consequence, more limited opportunities to attend university or train for particular careers). As part of her research into how social class can impact on student aspirations and educational and career opportunities, Jessie Abrahams visited three schools within one large city: an independent, fee-paying school; a high-performing and over-subscribed state school in one of the wealthiest parts of the city; and an undersubscribed state school in one of the most deprived areas in England (Abrahams, 2024).

In looking at the curriculum, Abrahams found that students at the school in the deprived area not only had a narrower range of subject choices at GCSE and A-level, but that a timetable blocking system also restricted which subjects they were able to choose. For example, pupils at both the independent school and the school in the deprived area had to choose a humanities subject, but the former could choose more than one from a list of seven (including Latin and Philosophy), while the latter could choose only history or geography (but not both). The grouping of other subjects under a blocking system at the school in the deprived area meant that students were unable to combine (for example) product design and drama, or IT and music. Whilst it is unreasonable to expect all schools to be able to offer unlimited subject options and combinations, it is also unreasonable that pupils can be so limited in their choices as a result of where they live.

Limited opportunities for social independence

In Chapter 4, we saw that for students entering higher education, the transition to study at undergraduate level can be more problematic for young people who for any number of reasons might choose to continue living in the family home and commute to university. Time and money spent travelling between home and study as well as less opportunity to join in with social occasions can make adapting to university life challenging for any student.

However, the impact of living at home is largest for students from a low-income background for whom restricted finances offer little chance for independence. This results in what Lorenza Antonucci refers to as a prolonged period of dependence (Antonucci, 2016); despite the availability of student finance, the high cost of living means that young people who should be beginning to transition to a state of independent adulthood whilst at university are unable to do so. Whilst young people from a wide range of backgrounds remain in a state of protracted semi-dependence during their university studies due to the 'in-limbo' nature of these years of study between childhood and full adulthood, Antonucci (2016) points out that structural factors play a huge role in postponing young people's transitions to adulthood and that, unfortunately, 'some young people have fewer resources to properly participate in HE' (p. 164).

Key takeaways:

- Schools in disadvantaged areas are often underfunded and understaffed compared to those in wealthier areas.
- Pupils who attend schools or colleges in disadvantaged areas may have a more limited choice of study options.
- University students from lower-income areas are more likely to live at the family home, limiting opportunities for social independence.

Case study: Local Matters

Local Matters is a collaborative research and training programme in which university-based academics work alongside headteachers and other school staff to explore what poverty looks like in their local area. The programme is based at the University of Manchester, and has been running across the north of England since 2017.

The programme consists of three phases. Firstly, members of staff from participating schools (normally one or two per school) attend taught sessions at the university to discuss localized data on poverty levels, as well as societal and governmental attitudes to poverty. Secondly, *all* staff at participating schools complete a survey in order to capture attitudes to poverty across the school from lunchtime supervisors to teaching assistants to school leaders. Finally, participants in the programme are supported in designing and implementing an action research project in their school, with the aim of making changes to policy and practice in order to support all students but particularly those from lower-income backgrounds.

Since the programme began, 975 members of school staff across the north of England have completed the attitudes to poverty survey. The rationale behind the survey is to start understanding how attitudes can shape our understanding of – and our responses to – poverty; after all, 'What we believe about students experiencing poverty and how we relate to them is as important as the mechanics of how we teach them; in fact, it plays a considerable role in determining how we teach them' (Gorski, 2018, p. 143). Bearing this in mind, some of the results to date suggest that pupils from lower-income backgrounds can face a serious disadvantage when moving to a new school and developing relationships with new school staff.

- 62 per cent of respondents strongly or somewhat agreed that 'At my school parents living in poverty are less likely to engage with their children's education'.
- 57 per cent strongly or somewhat disagreed that 'At my school families living in poverty have high aspirations'.
- 16 per cent agreed to at least some extent that 'At my school children living in poverty are less intelligent than other children'.

A recent evaluation of the Local Matters programme (Manchester Foodbank et al., 2024) interviewed previous and current participants and revealed some further insight into the challenges faced by students from lower-income backgrounds when transitioning to a new school. For example, one participant talked of how their school had come to better understand issues around clothing and uniforms as well as other potentially prohibitive costs, and as a result had implemented 'less non-uniform days, we have set up a second-hand uniform scheme, [and] ring-fenced spaces in our free sports clubs for our most vulnerable families' (Manchester Foodbank et al., 2024, p. 13). Such changes can help address challenges around building new relationships by eliminating stigma around clothing and facilitating social spaces in which to develop new friendships.

Elsewhere in the data, participants talked about the simple changes that could be made in the classroom in order to welcome all pupils, regardless of background. These could include changes to the school day in order to recognize that families may have complex work patterns, substantial caring responsibilities or challenges with travelling to school. One participant spoke of a school that

> has a soft start policy, where the gates are open at 8.40 and from 9 until 9.30 the children do an activity linked to the curriculum, but parents know they will be welcomed whenever they can arrive in that period. So dad might just be back from a nightshift and have to grab the kids off the doorstep to take them to school and might get stuck in traffic, but it just takes the pressure off. And if you sit in the foyer of that school you can feel the love and the welcome that the parents know they will get no matter what time they get there.
>
> (Manchester Foodbank et al., 2024, p. 14)

Participants also noted how important it was for children new to the school to see themselves reflected in the curriculum. A number of schools that took part in the programme adapted the content of their lessons in order to welcome and recognize all children from a particular area; for example, one school used local maps in a history lesson, 'looking at old and new to see how the area had changed … it's nice for the children to learn more about their area and to see it reflected in the curriculum they study' (Manchester Foodbank et al., 2024, p. 18). Placing a higher value on children's own local area also meant that schools could keep costs down for *all* children and parents, as trips could be organized to places within walking distance and which were free or minimal in cost. This approach views poverty through a lens of social justice rather than the deficit model that commonly appears in governmental and other discourses.

Key takeaways:

- School staff may hold negative attitudes towards students from lower-income backgrounds in terms of their intelligence and aspirations.
- Simple changes can be made to the school day to accommodate all students.
- Adapting the curriculum where possible means that schools can value and celebrate the communities and backgrounds of all pupils.

Implications for teaching and leadership staff

Concerns have quite rightly been raised over the increasing role that educational institutions, particularly schools, are being forced to play in combatting poverty and disadvantage in their local communities. For example, it is not uncommon for schools to give out food parcels and other material goods as well as providing free breakfast clubs and other forms of support for children and parents; in other words, 'informally acting as emergency food providers, welfare advisers, housing officers and social workers alongside their day jobs' (Butler, 2024, unpaged). It is important not to normalize this additional pressure on schools and those who work there, as this shifts responsibility away from government. However, the following advice may prove useful for supporting children and families from lower-income backgrounds.

School-based staff and leadership

- Look at ways to include pupils from all backgrounds in curriculum activities.
- Consider low-cost enrichment activities that are accessible for all pupils, particularly those which are within walking distance and showcase the local area.
- Use a range of activities to encourage parental involvement, and value the contributions that can be offered by families.
- Think about practical changes that can be made to reduce costs around uniforms and other essential school supplies, as well as small alterations to the school day that may make it easier for more children to attend.

College and university staff and leadership

- Work with families and students to understand the challenges faced around work and caring responsibilities.
- Be aware of the financial support available to students – such as hardship funds – and signpost encourage applications where appropriate.
- Be sympathetic to travel costs; for example, a one-to-one tutorial could be held online rather than have a student travel to campus for this one meeting.

Further reading

The impact of disadvantage on educational experiences and outcomes has been widely researched. Good places to start to find out more include publications by The Sutton Trust (https://www.suttontrust.com/about-us/) and The Joseph Rowntree Foundation (https://www.jrf.org.uk/).

References

Abrahams, J. (2024) *Schooling Inequality*. Bristol: Policy Press.
Andrew, A., Cattan, S., Costa-Dias, M., Farquharson, C., Kraftman, L., Krutikova, S., Phimister, A., & Sevilla, A. (2020) Learning during the lockdown: Real-time data on children's experiences during home learning. IFS: London. Available from: https://ifs.org.uk/sites/default/files/output_url_files/Edited_Final-BN288%252520Learning%252520during%252520the%252520lockdown.pdf.

Antonucci, L. (2016) *Student Lives in Crisis*. Bristol: Policy Press.

Butler, P. (2024) Teachers and GPs 'staggering' under extra demands caused by poverty in Great Britain. *Guardian*. Available from: https://www.theguardian.com/society/article/2024/jun/17/teachers-gps-staggering-extra-demands-poverty-great-britain#:~:text=Primary%20schools%20and%20GP%20services,relative%20poverty%20in%202022%2D23.

Cameron, D. (2012) Speech to conservative party conference. Available from: https://www.bbc.co.uk/news/av/uk-politics-19897855.

Department for Education (DfE) (2024a) Pupil premium: Overview. Available from: https://www.gov.uk/government/publications/pupil-premium/pupil-premium.

Department for Education (DfE) (2024b) Key stage 4 performance. Available from: https://explore-education-statistics.service.gov.uk/find-statistics/key-stage-4-performance/2022-23.

Devine, B. (2023) Available from: https://researchbriefings.files.parliament.uk/documents/SN07096/SN07096.pdf.

Drummond, M.J., & Yarker, P. (2013) The enduring problem of fixed ability: But is a new conversation beginning? *FORUM: For Promoting 3–19 Comprehensive Education*, 55(1), 3–7.

Explore Education Statistics (2024) Pupil absence in schools in England (academic year 2022/23). Available from: https://explore-education-statistics.service.gov.uk/find-statistics/pupil-absence-in-schools-in-england/2022-23.

Gillborn, D. (2006) Rethinking white supremacy: Who counts in 'White World'. *Ethnicities*, 6(3), 318–40.

Gorski, P.C. (2018) *Reaching and Teaching Students in Poverty: Strategies for Erasing the Opportunity Gap*. 2nd ed. Columbia: Teachers College Press.

Gregory, E. (2022) The effects of disadvantage. In: Lord, J. ed., *Psychology of Education: Theory, Research and Evidence-Based Practice* (pp. 345–62). London: SAGE.

Howker, E., & Black, L. (forthcoming) The role of everyday mathematics in parent and caregiver experiences of alienation from school mathematics. Special issue on Parents, Caregivers and Community in Mathematics Education in *Educational Studies in Mathematics*.

Manchester Central Foodbank, Gregory, E., & Clare, S. (2024) An evaluation of the local matters participatory research and teaching programme: How has the participatory methodology worked and what has been the impact on education policy and practice? University of Manchester evaluation report. Unpublished. Executive summary available from: display.aspx.

May, T. (2016) Britain, the great meritocracy: Prime Minister's speech. Available from: https://www.gov.uk/government/speeches/britain-the-great-meritocracy-prime-ministers-speech.

Office for National Statistics (ONS) (2024) Cost of living latest insights. Available from: https://www.ons.gov.uk/economy/inflationandpriceindices/articles/costofliving/latestinsights.

Reay, D. (2024) If pupils avoid school due to anxiety, the system needs to change. *Guardian*. 7 February. Available from: https://www.theguardian.com/education/2024/feb/07/if-pupils-avoid-school-due-to-anxiety-the-system-needs-to-change.

Sutton Trust (2023) Cost of living and university students. Available from: https://www.suttontrust.com/our-research/cost-of-living-and-university-students-2023/.

UK Parliament (2021) School funding. Available from: https://publications.parliament.uk/pa/cm5802/cmselect/cmpubacc/183/18302.htm.

Index

absenteeism (from school) 94, 123, 136, 168
academic change during transitions 4, 24, 43, 95, 129, 148
additional support needs
   disability and health needs 77, 94, 105, 128
   English as an Additional Language (EAL) 14, 43, 77
   social and emotional factors 10–11, 24, 35, 77, 145, 157
age at transition 82
A-Level 57–60, 62, 69–71, 174
anxiety (*see also* mental health)
   heighten levels of 58, 61, 64, 76, 84, 97, 115
   lower levels of 26, 63, 82, 101
   manifestation of 137
   social 130, 134
assessment
   baseline assessments 10, 48
   formative 97, 134–5
   high stakes testing 11, 62, 115–16
   of attainment 25, 70
   phonics screening 3, 28
   risk 105
   standardized testing 167, 170
   statutory 8–9, 49
   summative 97, 135
   Teacher 48
   types of 63
attendance (*see also* absenteeism)
   decline in 79, 94–5
   full-time 4
   increase 115–16
   of parents 111, 121
   part-time 16–17
   regular 60, 101
   non 69, 101
austerity 165
autism 77, 106
awarding gap 171

behaviour
   challenging 95, 97, 132
   expectations of 130–1, 135, 137, 141
   impact of 115, 127–8, 130
   management 117, 143, 150, 153, 157
   online 136
   school policies 128–9, 137–40, 142, 144
BTECs 58–9, 62–3, 69–70

case studies
   behaviour-related 137
   in early years 105
   in primary 33–4, 85, 105, 137
   in secondary 46, 49, 85, 105
   Local Matters 175
   parental engagement 119
   post-16 68
   SEND- related 105
   Talking about School Transition 5–7 152
child-led learning 5–6
classroom
   layout 26, 31–2
   number and location 52
   provision 32, 34, 96, 101, 107
   routines 35, 60, 132
   rules and codes of conducts 53, 114
   strategies 138, 141–3
collaborative approaches 13, 23, 33
College
   of Further Education 57, 66, 68
   sixth form 57, 59, 64, 66–7, 71
communication
   between schools 14, 33, 98, 122, 159
   skills 24
   with parents 14, 25, 33, 102, 116–17, 122
community
   local 12–13, 119–20, 122
   partnerships 3, 15
   school 8, 13, 127, 138, 142, 144
continuous provision 25, 31, 35, 37, 100

Covid-19, impact of 77, 94, 98–9, 114, 129, 141, 151
culture, school 127–8, 135–9, 142
curriculum
    emotional-centred transition curriculum 147
    extracurricular activities 172
    Talking about School Transition 5–7 curriculum 147, 152–4

Department for Education (DfE)
    behaviour 129
    careers 70
    EYFS 24, 27–8
    Pupil Premium 112
    pupil progress 48, 151, 171
    Schools, Pupils and Their Characteristics 50
    SEND 42, 94–95, 103
    Teacher Standards 42
    'Wasted Years' 42, 44
disability 77, 105
disadvantage
    definition 166
    impact on attainment 171, 178
    impact on engagement 112
    Pupil Premium 173

Early Years Education
    types of providers 23
Early Years Foundation Stage (EYFS)
    assessment 3, 6, 8, 10–12, 22–3, 27–9, 38
    framework 4, 6, 24, 38
    implementation of 4, 23, 27
    introduction of 3, 7
Education Endowment Foundation (EEF) 112, 130, 143, 145
Education, Health and Care Plan (EHCPs) 95, 99–100, 102–4, 106–7
employment
    part-time whilst studying 168
    transitions into 93, 103
English as an additional language (EAL) (*see* additional support needs)
Establish-Maintain-Restore (EMR) method, the 131
'Every Child Matters' 128
exclusions 94, 102, 115

family/school relationships 8, 13, 132
feedback
    to parents 133
    to pupils 62, 134–5
formative assessment 62, 97, 134–5
Free School Meals (FSM) 43, 166, 168, 171–2
friendship 35, 80, 82, 87, 130, 172, 176

GCSE
    definition 42, 58–9
    journey through 71, 113, 170–1
    structure of 62–3, 96, 117
gender, impact of on transitions 85, 173

homework
    amount of 79, 134, 169
    support with 169
    types of 60, 78

inclusion 34–6, 95–6, 103, 122
independence
    independent learning 60–1, 169
    independent living 103
induction 35–6, 41, 47, 53–4
inequalities
    in accessing provision 57, 111, 166
    in educational outcomes 120
    of representation 118, 166
    social 150
International perspectives of transition
    Australia 76, 82–3
    Denmark 82
    Germany 81
    Israel 82
    Scotland 76–7, 81, 84–5
    United States 78, 82–4, 148–9, 154

key stages
    EYFS: *See Early Years Foundation Stage*
    KS1 21, 24–6, 28, 30, 34–5, 49, 107
    KS2 22, 41–9, 151
    KS3 22, 41–6, 113, 115, 151
    KS4 22, 41, 58, 95, 115
    KS5 59, 117
knowledge
    gaps in 49
    of pathways 70

pastoral 17, 42, 118, 151, 157
professional 9–11, 25, 143, 160
Pupils' knowledge of curriculum 10, 22, 24, 44–6, 59, 67, 167, 170
Pupils' knowledge of transition processes 156–9

learning goals 134
legislation
    Children and Families Act (UK) (2014) 94–5
    Equality Act (UK) (2010) 93, 95
    Individuals with Disabilities Education Act (US) (IDEA 2004) 78
    SEND Code of Practice (UK) (2015) 93
    The Education (Additional Support for Learning) (Scotland) Act (2004) (amended 2009) 77
local authorities, responsibilities of 77, 84, 94, 152, 158, 160
lockdowns, impact of 168–9
low socio-economic status 118, 121

mainstream education (and SEND pupils) 96, 103–5, 148
mental health
    'Mental Health and Behaviour in Schools' (UK Government guidance) 128
multicultural 128
Multiple and multi-dimensional transitions theory (MMT) 80, 154

National Curriculum, the 24–6, 42–3, 49, 59, 129, 167

Ofsted 6, 42, 44, 137–8, 151
online learning 23, 61–3, 114, 178

parental engagement
    impact of 112–15, 122, 138
    in rural communities 111, 119–20
    with immigrant families 112, 120
peer pressure 131, 134, 136–7, 172
Personal, Social, Health and Economic Education (PSHE) 129–30, 159
phonics 3, 6, 28

play
    in early years 5, 9–10, 24–5
    in primary 26, 31–4, 37, 100, 107, 170
post-16 education 57–9, 62–72
pre-school settings (*see Early Years Education*)
primary education 49, 100, 102, 134
Pupil Premium 112, 159, 166, 173

qualifications
    A-Level 57–60, 62, 69–71, 174
    availability of 66, 68, 71
    BTEC 58–9, 62–3, 69–70
    GCSE
        definition 42, 58–9
        journey through 71–2, 113, 170–1
        structure of 62–3, 96, 117
    SATs 28, 47–9, 54, 96, 155, 167
    T-Level 59–60
    vocational 58–60, 62–4, 66, 69–70

reception baseline assessment 8, 10–12, 29–30
relationships
    with parents 8, 112, 115–16, 122, 138, 156
    with peers 81, 172
    with teachers 64, 80, 84
research into transitions challenges of 75

SATs 28, 47–9, 54, 96, 155, 167
school(s)
    climate 84
    culture 127–8, 135–9, 142
    leadership 17
    location of 14
    middle schools 50, 82, 148–9
    nurseries 4, 16–17, 21–3, 27, 105
    primary 12, 30, 45, 50, 86, 98, 131, 145, 158
    secondary 41, 44, 87, 101–2, 112, 117, 131, 167
    size of 83, 156
    structure of 82
    types of 12, 148–9
secondary education 45, 66, 101, 113, 116, 118
SENCO, role of 33, 47, 93

social change during transitions 64, 75, 166
social mobility 67, 166–7
socioeconomic status (*see also* disadvantage) 43, 71
special educational needs
    accessing mainstream schools 95–6, 104
    additional support for 77–8, 84, 104, 159–60
    annual review 100, 103–7
    information and paperwork 97–8
    labelling 171
    SEND Code of Practice (2015) 93
statutory guidance 3, 10, 23
Steer Report, the 128
student(s)
    higher risk students 95, 114, 150, 152, 157, 159, 168, 171
    home students 58, 67
    international students 58–9
    living at home 67, 174
    widening participation students 72
summative assessment 135
suspensions 94, 102, 115

Talking about School Transition 5–7 (TaST) 147, 152–4
teacher(s)
    different relationship with 64, 75, 80
    number of different teachers 51–2
technology, use of
    for independent work 169
    to support transition 102, 104, 116

tests (*see* assessment)
T-Levels 59–60
transition
    days 28, 35–6
    from childhood to adulthood 64, 103, 174–5
    from EYFS to primary 21, 25–26, 30–1, 35
    from home to early schooling 1, 7, 11, 13, 16, 98, 105
    from primary to secondary 41–2, 45, 49, 52, 93, 95, 101, 105
    from secondary to post-16 57, 59, 63–4, 66, 111, 170
    international perspectives 75
    processes 13, 104, 111, 123
    risk factors 81, 152, 157, 160
    to university 65, 69
    to work 62–63, 69

university
    accommodation 65
    admissions 66
    awarding gap 171
    drop-out rates 76
    post-1992 universities 67
    Russell Group universities 66–7

vocational education 58–60, 62–64, 66, 69–70

well-being, emotional 30, 35, 147, 150–60